TASTE
OF
NEW YORK

TASTE OF NEW YORK

SIGNATURE DISHES OF THE BEST RESTAURANTS

KAREN GANTZ ZAHLER

PHOTOGRAPHS BY
TOM ECKERLE

♦

ADDISON-WESLEY PUBLISHING COMPANY

Reading, Massachusetts   Menlo Park, California   New York
Don Mills, Ontario   Wokingham, England   Amsterdam   Bonn
Sydney   Singapore   Tokyo   Madrid   San Juan
Paris   Seoul   Milan   Mexico City   Taipei

Library of Congress Cataloging-in-Publication Data

Zahler, Karen Gantz.
      Taste of New York : signature dishes of the best restaurants /
Karen Gantz Zahler ; photographs by Tom Eckerle.
      p.   cm.
    Includes index.
    ISBN 0-201-62208-4
    1. Cookery, American.   2. Cookery, International.   3. Cookery—
New York (N.Y.)   4. Restaurants—New York (N.Y.)   I. Title.
TX715.Z28   1993
641.59—dc20   93-176
                                                              CIP

Prop styling by Francine Matalon-Degni and Ceci Gallini
Food styling by Roscoe Betsill, William Smith, and Rick Ellis

Text design by Barbara Cohen Aronica
Jacket design by Diana Coe and Jean Seal
Set in 11¹/₂-point Bembo by Pagesetters, Inc., Brattleboro, VT

1 2 3 4 5 6 7 8 9-DO-9796959493
First printing, August 1993

To Eric, for the love I always dreamed of.

To Pat and Manny, for their noble inspiration.

CONTENTS

ACKNOWLEDGMENTS

I am greatly indebted to my husband, Eric Zahler; my sisters, Kim and Kathy Gantz; JoAnn and Robert Bendetson; my parents, Patricia and Emanuel Gantz; and my friends for being discerning judges of these formidable creations and providing the moral support needed to undertake such a culinary journey.

I gratefully acknowledge the guidance and support of my editor, Elizabeth Carduff; the editorial assistance of Joan Hughes, Toni Rachiele, and Evie Righter; the assistance of John Fuller, Len Gilbert, and Pat Jalbert; and the patience of Carol Lynn Carlson, for typing the manuscript.

For their invaluable suggestions, I thank most sincerely and affectionately John Agresto, Leon Jacobson, Steve Honigman, Rhonda Kirshner, Bob Lape, Ellis Levine, Judith Miller, and Howard Siegel.

My deepest gratitude to Miriam Brickman and Jean-Jacques Rachou for helping me master French culinary techniques.

I pay particular homage to the following chefs for their invaluable assistance and for sharing their skills and time: Jay Cohen, Bobby Flay, Frederic Heba, and Jean Louis Montrecot. Also, my deep gratitude to the following chefs, restaurant proprietors, and managers: Hitch Albin, Francesco Antonucci, Peter Aschkenasy, Umberto and Vittorio Assante, Stephano Bastiani, Lidia Bastianich, Giorgio Bottazzi, Antoine Bouterin, Wayne Harley Brachman, Terrance Brennan, Georges Briguet, Edward Brown, Dan Budd, David Burke, Jean Robert de Cavel, Dominique Cerrone, Guy Cesina, Alan Chan, Kawal Jit Singh Chandhoke, Kate Chorlton, Harry Cipriani, Nicola Civetta, Tom Collichio, Andrew Cotton, Andrew D'Amico, Jean-Michel Diot, Tom Eagan, Thomas Ferlesch, Larry Forgione, Virgilio Gatti, Adi Giovannetti, Eric Gouteyron, Carlos Guiseppi, John Halligan, Josephina Howard, Gary Jacobson, Morgan Jacobson, André and Rita Jammet, Nicola Jovic, Peter Klein, Gray Kunz, Christer Larsson, Patrick Lemblé, Eileen and Larry Leong, Sarabeth and Bill Levine, Michael Lomonaco, Richard Lopuzzo, John Loughran, Sirio and Mario Maccioni, Waldy Malouf, Fernando Masci, Masaei Seki, Danny Meyer, Frank Minieri, Tadashi Ono, Charles Palmer, Debra Ponzek, José Ramone, Seppi Renggli, Hervé Riou, Michael Romano, Anne Rosenzweig, Frank Rossini, Tony Rossini, Henny Santo, Richard Schloss, André Soltner, Sandy Tang, Natalie Tennenbaum, Kostas Teryetis, Bruno Tison, Michael Tong, Pablo Trobo, Romy Vega, Jean-Georges Vongerichten, David Waltog, David Waltuck, Barry Wine, and Eduardo Ynaim.

I acknowledge the following purveyors for the exceptional quality of their food: F. Rozzo & Sons and Piccinini's Meat Market. I also wish to thank Bridge Kitchenware Corporation for the integrity of their products.

My special thanks to Wendy Schneider for her styling advice, and Jean and Christopher Angell, Camilla and Jean Bergeron, Tom Britt, Mario Buatta, Lilly and William O'Boyle, Andrea and John Stark, Jeanette Solomon, Alison Spear, and Vivian Weissman for providing the fine antique china, table settings, and flower bouquets that give my book a majestic touch.

INTRODUCTION

Taste of New York unlocks the most closely guarded secrets of New York's superstar chefs and food luminaries. I prepared these culinary gems with chefs in over 75 restaurant kitchens and tested and demystified them for home use. I also interviewed chefs, restaurant proprietors, food writers, and restaurant enthusiasts to identify the chefs' signature dishes—those creations reflecting their personal vision of cooking. For example, David Burke, chef at the Park Avenue Cafe, produces a dramatic carrot cake soufflé with a sumptuous cream cheese filling cascading from its center. He transforms the classic French dessert into a contemporary American temptation incorporating carrot cake ingredients and wrapping the soufflé with phyllo dough.

Taste of New York celebrates New York, the city with the finest cuisine in the United States, a culinary tradition that transcends ethnic and regional boundaries and challenges the world's great food meccas. New York is a cosmopolitan and cultured world in itself, a way of life, a city that attracts artists, lawyers, doctors, and international entrepreneurs. The city is a magnet for such talent and has responded to their discerning palates.

Food is inextricably woven into New York's heritage and vitality. The city's diverse culture, as well as its economic and intellectual resources, fosters a level of refinement stressing every detail of the food, from the place settings and decorative china to the aromatic blossoms gracing the table. The character of the food, the nuances of taste, the quality of ingredients, and presentation constitute a distinct art form. New York is a master at celebrating food as art. As noted architect Mies Van der Rohe instructed: "God is in the details."

A revolution in cooking has been taking place in New York, fueled by the growing abundance of fresh ingredients from around the country and abroad. Arugula and *broccoli rabe* have been transplanted from the pushcarts of Little Italy to Il Cantinori and The '21' Club. Lemongrass perfumes not only the grocers' stalls in Chinatown, but also the Seafood Steamed in Bamboo with Savoy Cabbage at The Sea Grill in Rockefeller Center. New York chefs collaborate with farmers to custom-grow ingredients, and farmers' markets and specialty food shops are responding to the ingredients explosion. Asian spices tempt our palates and abound on restaurant menus. Focusing on lighter fare, chefs are replacing puff pastry with phyllo dough, and cream with infused oils, fruit sauces and purées. But even the revolution in health consciousness has not tamed New Yorkers' passion for chocolate confections and other epicurean indulgences; witness such dazzling yet easy-to-prepare desserts as Le Cirque's *Crème Brûlée* and The Four Seasons' Raspberry Summer Pudding.

My own culinary interest stems from my good fortune in having pursued high school studies in France where, in addition to probing French poetry and Renaissance literature, I mastered the basics of Lyonnaise cuisine. I returned home with an enriched culinary repertoire ranging from pike *quenelles* and crusty *galettes Pérougiennes* to *Gruyère* soufflés and rabbit stew.

My earliest culinary interest was awakened by my mother. From her I learned to create and appreciate dishes as varied as *ratatouille, blinis,* and *coeurs à la crème.* Our family table has always been a celebration of joyous events, a forum for conversation, expressions of support, the exchange of ideas, and all the real treasures of family life. As Samuel Pepys, the great chronicler of Charles II's regime, aptly noted: "Strange to see how a good dinner and feasting reconciles everybody."

Taste of New York is written for home entertainers who enjoy creating and sharing great food with family and friends. I have had the privilege of cooking with some of New York's master chefs, among them Frederic Heba, former executive *chef de cuisine* of La Grenouille, Jay Cohen, *sous chef* at Bouley, and Jean Louis Montrecot, *sous chef* at La Côte Basque. These experiences, in addition to my apprecticeships in New York restaurants—notably La Côte Basque and Le Cirque—have helped me grow as a cook and have heightened my appreciation of the subtle artistry and discipline that combine to create memorable food.

I hope *Taste of New York* inspires you to delight in New York's most spectacular culinary secrets.

—Karen Gantz Zahler

Jerry Ruotolo

*Author Karen Gantz Zahler
and Chef Seppi Renggli in the
kitchen of The Sea Grill*

TASTE
OF
NEW YORK

APPETIZERS

Crusty, grilled Italian peasant bread brushed with olive oil and garlic has become the rage in New York, and Il Mulino serves bruschetta *at its best. Topped with marinated tomato, basil, and sweet onion, this* bruschetta *is seasoned to perfection.*

TOMATO-BASIL BRUSCHETTA

IL MULINO

4 ripe tomatoes, cored

2 branches basil, stems removed and finely julienned

1 tablespoon Italian parsley, finely chopped

1/2 purple onion, peeled and finely chopped

3 shallots, peeled and finely chopped

1/2 teaspoon sea salt

1/2 teaspoon freshly ground black pepper

1 1/2 cups olive oil

1/2 cup water

1 teaspoon chopped fresh oregano

1 tablespoon red wine vinegar

1 small round loaf of Italian bread

3 garlic cloves, peeled

1. Chop the tomatoes with skin and seeds into 1/4-inch cubes and place in a large bowl. Add the basil, parsley, onion and shallots. Season with salt and pepper to taste. Pour in olive oil, water, oregano, and vinegar and marinate for 3 hours at room temperature. Refrigerate prior to serving.

2. Toast 1-inch-thick slices of Italian bread and when hot, rub top sides with whole garlic cloves.

3. When ready to serve, spoon a generous amount of the tomato-basil mixture over the bread.

SERVES 4

CAPONATA

DA UMBERTO

1/2 cup plus 3 tablespoons extra-virgin
   olive oil

2 large eggplants, cut into 3/4-inch cubes

4 tablespoons kosher salt

4 garlic cloves, peeled and chopped

1 cup tomato sauce (follow the Penne
   All'Arrabbiata sauce instructions, page
   77)

1 1/2 tablespoons white vinegar

1 tablespoon sugar

1 tablespoon capers

5 green olives, pitted and sliced

1/2 stalk celery, chopped

salt and freshly ground black pepper to
   taste

3 anchovy filets, finely chopped

3 fresh basil leaves, stemmed and
   chopped

3 tablespoons Italian parsley, chopped

Caponata, *the classic accompaniment to capon, is one of the great Sicilian culinary legacies, and is served as an antipasto as well as a side dish.*

   Da Umberto, the quintessential Italian trattoria, *distinguishes itself with a stunning assortment of antipasti.*

1. Heat 1/2 cup olive oil in a large sauté pan, add the eggplant, and sauté for 4 to 5 minutes. Remove the eggplant to paper towels to drain and sprinkle with kosher salt to extract the water. Cover the eggplants with a layer of paper towels and place a heavy pan on top of them for approximately 3 hours.

2. In a large, deep saucepan, heat 3 tablespoons of olive oil. When hot, add the chopped garlic and sauté for 2 minutes. Then add the tomato sauce and cook for 5 minutes, or until the mixture starts to bubble. Add the white vinegar, sugar, capers, olives, and celery. Season with salt and pepper to taste and simmer, covered, over low heat until the sauce thickens. Add the eggplant and anchovies and simmer until the mixture is heated through. Add basil and parsley and combine. Let cool to room temperature before serving.

SERVES 7

The culinary creations of Anne Rosenzweig, one of the stars of innovative American cuisine, are known for their inspired and contrasting flavors and textures. These savory yellow corn cakes, topped with a generous dollop of crème fraîche, are then regally adorned with two caviars. They are perfectly suited for the likes of Arcadia, which in Greek mythology is a land of pastoral beauty and splendor. They are the ultimate amuse-bouche, or teaser to "amuse the mouth" before the entrée is served.

CORN CAKES WITH CREME FRAICHE AND CAVIARS

ARCADIA

1 1/2 cups fresh corn kernels
1/2 cup milk
1/3 cup yellow cornmeal
1/3 cup flour
4 tablespoons sweet butter, melted
2 eggs
2 egg yolks
salt to taste
1/2 teaspoon freshly ground black pepper
1/2 cup Clarified Butter (page 196)

GARNISH
1/2 cup Crème Fraîche (page 196) or sour cream
8 tablespoons golden whitefish caviar
4 tablespoons sevruga caviar
1/4 cup chopped fresh chives

1. Make the corn cakes: Roughly chop the corn kernels either with a knife or in a food processor until creamy but still chunky in consistency. Place the corn in a large bowl and whisk in the milk, cornmeal, and flour until there are no lumps. In another bowl, whisk together the melted butter, eggs, and egg yolks. Stir in the corn mixture and season with salt, pepper, and half the chives.

2. Heat the clarified butter in a large skillet over medium heat. Ladle 2 tablespoons of the corn cake mixture into the pan so that each cake is the size of a silver dollar. Cook the corn cakes until they are golden brown, then flip them and continue cooking until they are golden on the second side. Repeat this process until all the batter has been used. To keep the corn cakes warm before serving, place them in a preheated 350 degree F. oven.

3. To serve, place 4 overlapping corn cakes on each plate. Garnish each serving with a dollop of crème fraîche, golden caviar, and then top that with the sevruga caviar and a sprinkling of the remaining chopped chives.

SERVES 8

This extraordinarily ambitious hors d'œuvre is visually stunning and sensuously delicious. Luscious pearls of caviar are enveloped in moist crepes that are then tied with delicate chive ribbons. Perched gracefully on candlesticks, these majestic purses are topped with edible gold leaf, a garnish used for centuries by Roman, Mogul, and Renaissance hosts.

CREPES TIED WITH CHIVES AND FILLED WITH CAVIAR

Beggars' Purses

THE QUILTED GIRAFFE

2 cups pastry flour

pinch of salt

3 cups milk, at room temperature

8 whole eggs

1 egg yolk

2¹/₂ tablespoons Clarified Butter

   (page 196)

24 green chives

¹/₄ cup Crème Fraîche

   (page 196)

1¹/₄ cups beluga caviar

24 thin slices of lime

OPTIONAL

edible gold leaf

1. Make the crepes: In a stainless steel bowl, combine the flour and salt with 1 cup of the milk. Whisk until a paste forms and all lumps are removed. Whisk in the remaining milk, eggs, and egg yolk until smooth. Let the batter rest, covered with plastic wrap, for 1 hour.

2. Stir the batter, then strain it through a fine sieve into a bowl sitting in a bath of warm water, a *bain-marie*. Stir the batter until it is warm to the touch. Whisk in the warm clarified butter.

3. Using a 2-ounce ladle, pour the batter into a well-seasoned 4-inch-wide cast-iron crepe pan (see Note). Quickly move the batter around to coat the bottom of the pan; return any excess batter to the bowl in the *bain-marie*. Cook the crepes until the edges start to release from the pan. Turn the pan at an angle and, using the tip of the paring knife and your fingers, remove the crepe to a flat surface. Stack the crepes one on top of the other, cooked side down. Immediately wrap them tightly in plastic wrap and refrigerate until ready to use.

4. Blanch the chives in a pot of boiling salted water over high heat by stirring them quickly until submerged, approximately 10 to 20 seconds. Shock the chives in very cold water to stop the cooking process. Dry on a towel.

5. Bring the crepes to room temperature and place them on top of each other on a piece of parchment or wax paper. Use the top of a 500-gram caviar tin or 4³/₄-inch round cutter and a knife to trim the edges.

6. Place 1 teaspoon of *crème fraîche* in the center of each crepe. Spoon 1 tablespoon caviar on each dollop of *crème fraîche*. Carefully holding the edge of

the crepe farthest away from you between your forefinger and thumb, use your free hand to make small, even pleats in the edge of the crepe, catching each pleat between your forefinger and thumb. Pleat the last section and tie the crepe closed with a single chive in a double knot. Trim all but ¹/₂ inch off the chive ends.

7. Refrigerate the crepe purses until ready to serve. Before serving, brush the top of each with a small amount of warm clarified butter. To serve, arrange each crepe purse on a slice of lime, and top with gold leaf if desired. Allow 3 crepes per person.

N O T E :   The most difficult part of this recipe is making the crepes. While a nonstick pan can be used, a seasoned crepe pan is preferable. To season your pan, warm it in a 300 degree F. oven for 15 minutes. Then fill it two-thirds of the way up the sides with clarified butter. Let the pan stand at room temperature filled with butter for 10 to 15 minutes. Carefully pour off the butter, then wipe the pan dry with paper towels. After the crepes are made, wipe out the pan with 1 teaspoon kosher salt and a paper towel, removing excess batter. Once the pan has been seasoned, do not wash it with soap and water.

S E R V E S   8

*Jean-Georges Vongerichten's
simple, intensely flavored cuisine
relies upon juices, vinaigrettes,
infused oils, and broths instead of
stocks and cream sauces. Although
flavored oils have been used in the
cooking of southwestern France,
Jean-Georges pioneered their use in
America, and his approach has
won an enthusiastic following
among American chefs and culinary
enthusiasts alike.*

*In this savory terrine, the
arugula juice, coarse salt, and
cracked pepper provide a pleasing
contrast to the creamy consistency of
the goat cheese. The seasoning is
an important aspect of the texture
of this dish.*

GOAT CHEESE AND POTATO TERRINE WITH ARUGULA JUICE

JO JO

4 large Idaho potatoes
¼ cup Clarified Butter (page 196)
3½ logs goat cheese, 11 ounces each, at
    room temperature
3 sprigs thyme with flowers attached

ARUGULA JUICE
1 bunch arugula, washed and patted dry
1 cup extra-virgin olive oil
1 pound mesclun (mixed greens),
    washed and patted dry

½ CUP DRESSING
2 tablespoons fresh lemon juice
pinch of salt
pinch of freshly ground black pepper
¼ cup extra-virgin olive oil
1½ teaspoons boiling water

GARNISH
coarse salt to taste
freshly ground cracked black pepper to
    taste
3 tablespoons chopped chives

1. Preheat the oven to 325 degrees F.

2. Peel the potatoes and slice them thinly lengthwise. Brush the potatoes on both sides with clarified butter. (The potatoes must be cooked immediately or they will turn black.) Place individual potato slices in a single layer on a nonstick baking sheet and bake for 12 to 15 minutes. Place the cooked potatoes on a cloth towel and pat them dry.

3. Wet the inside of an 11- × 4-inch terrine pan with water, and line it with wax paper. Arrange a layer of potatoes lengthwise over the bottom of the terrine, overlapping the slices slightly. Then line both sides of the terrine with potato slices, standing them upright, with the thicker end of the slices touching the rim. Press the potatoes down so that they stay in place. Reserve remaining potatoes to fill terrine.

4. Flatten the goat cheese logs into an even layer with your fingertips. Place half of the flattened goat cheese in the terrine and press it down with the palms of your hands.

5. Sprinkle some of the crushed flower parts of the thyme sprigs over the goat cheese. Arrange a second lengthwise layer of potatoes to cover the thyme. Add another layer of goat cheese and sprinkle with the thyme. Fold the tops of the potato slices lining the sides over the cheese. Cover the terrine with plastic wrap. This will enable the mold to set and facilitate its removal from the pan. Place a weight (such as another terrine pan) on top of the plastic wrap and refrigerate for 2 hours before serving.

6. Make the arugula juice: Place well-cleaned arugula through a juice extractor twice. Place the arugula juice in an airtight jar and mix in the olive oil. Store refrigerated until ready to use.

7. Make the dressing: Place the lemon juice and a pinch each of salt and pepper in a small food processor or blender and add oil. Process for 30 seconds. Add boiling water and process for an additional 10 seconds. Pour into an airtight jar and refrigerate until ready to use.

8. To serve, unmold the terrine by inverting it. Cut it into 12 slices. Toss the *mesclun* with the dressing in a bowl and portion them around the top half of each dinner plate. Place a slice of the terrine in the center of each plate and spoon the arugula juice around it. Generously season each slice with coarse salt and freshly ground black pepper to taste and sprinkle with chives.

HINTS FROM THE CHEF: The potatoes should remain on the cloth (Step 2) for no more than 15 to 20 minutes; otherwise the starch in them will leak and cause them to stick. The terrine can be made in advance and refrigerated for up to 3 days. In order to extract the juice from vegetables, you need to use a juice extractor; food processors and citrus juicers do not adequately separate the juice from the pulp. Herb oils such as basil, chervil, or parsley can be processed in a blender.

SERVES 12

LETTUCE WRAP WITH MINCED SQUAB

CANTON

1/2 head iceberg lettuce

2 tablespoons peanut oil

2 garlic cloves, peeled and crushed

2 1/3 teaspoons salt

1 pound finely ground skinless squab, pork loin, or chicken

1/2 pound fresh water chestnuts, minced

1/4 pound canned bamboo shoots, minced

6 tablespoons shelled fresh green peas

2 tablespoons soy sauce

1 tablespoon sherry

6 tablespoons oyster sauce

pinch of white pepper

1 tablespoon sesame oil, optional

hoisin sauce

1. Soak the lettuce in a bowl of ice-cold water for 10 to 15 minutes. Separate the leaves and place them in a colander to drip dry.

2. Heat the peanut oil in a wok and when hot, brown the garlic. Season with salt, then remove and discard the garlic.

3. In the wok, stir-fry the meat until brown. Add water chestnuts, bamboo shoots, and peas, and continue to stir-fry with continuous movements for a few minutes. Spread the meat out and press down on it with a metal spatula. Add the soy sauce and sherry. Brown over high heat for approximately 1 minute. Add oyster sauce, white pepper, and sesame oil, if using, and stir until combined completely. Press the meat down with the spatula and stir again.

4. To serve, place several leaves of lettuce on each plate. Spoon 1 1/2 tablespoons of the filling in the center of each leaf, then roll it up into the shape of a cigar. Arrange on the platter seam-side down and serve with hoisin sauce.

NOTE: Hoisin sauce is an oyster-flavored sauce available at oriental markets.

SERVES 4

MUSHROOMS WITH ARUGULA

IL CANTINORI

4 bunches arugula, stemmed

2 pounds shiitake *mushrooms and oyster mushrooms combined*

4 tablespoons extra-virgin olive oil

3 garlic cloves, peeled and sliced

salt and freshly ground black pepper to taste

2 tablespoons balsamic vinegar

1. Clean the arugula well, pat dry, and set aside.

2. Clean the mushrooms with a damp towel and cut them in half.

3. Heat 3 tablespoons of the olive oil in a large sauté pan until piping hot, add the garlic cloves, and brown them. Add the mushrooms and salt and pepper to taste. When the mushrooms are reduced in size and cooked until tender—approximately 8 minutes—drain off the excess oil. Return the pan to the stove, add 1 tablespoon balsamic vinegar to the mushrooms, and combine.

4. Place the arugula in a bowl and toss with the remaining olive oil and vinegar.

5. To serve, place arugula in the center of each plate and top with mushrooms.

SERVES 4

The secret to these simple yet flavorful, aromatic mushrooms is the final splash of balsamic vinegar that gives them their pungency.

With its luxurious potted plants, white stucco walls, terra-cotta floors, and wood-beamed ceilings, Il Cantinori is as close to Tuscany as you will find in New York City. Renowned for its upscale Tuscan home cooking, Il Cantinori reflects the strong agricultural traditions of the region.

This flavorful, rosemary-scented lobster and creamy-textured potato mixture with provençale represents a complex rendering of textures and flavors. Drizzled with a luscious veal sauce, these lobster timbales are a sensation for any dinner party.

After three decades of business, the legendary La Côte Basque is still one of the city's grandest restaurants. The walls are covered with breathtaking murals of the Basque sea town of Saint-Jean-de-Luz, creating the illusion that you are dining in a thatched-roof house by the sea.

LOBSTER TIMBALE WITH ROSEMARY SAUCE

LA COTE BASQUE

$1^1/_3$ quarts heavy cream

5 large Idaho potatoes, peeled and thinly sliced

1 cup shallots, peeled and sliced

1 teaspoon salt

1 cup white vinegar

2 pounds lobster meat (3 lobsters, 1 pound each)

$^1/_2$ cup extra-virgin olive oil

1 pound sea scallops, sliced in half horizontally

1 tablespoon mixed chopped fresh tarragon, thyme, and chives

ROSEMARY SAUCE

1 tablespoon sweet butter

3 shallots, peeled and sliced

2 cups Brown Veal Stock (page 207)

1 small sprig fresh rosemary

2 tablespoons sweet butter

$^1/_2$ teaspoon freshly ground white pepper to taste

PROVENCALE

6 plum tomatoes

5 large tomatoes

1 tablespoon olive oil

3 shallots, peeled and thinly sliced

1 garlic clove, peeled and sliced

2 bay leaves

1 sprig fresh thyme

$^1/_2$ bunch basil leaves

6 whole basil leaves for garnish

OPTIONAL

1 teaspoon olive oil

1 pound shrimp, peeled and deveined

1 pound sea scallops

1 teaspoon sweet butter

salt and freshly ground white pepper to taste

1. In a large saucepan, cook the heavy cream, potatoes, and 1 cup of shallots over medium heat for 30 minutes. Stir frequently with a wooden spoon to prevent sticking. Strain the mixture through a mesh sieve into a large bowl.

2. Cook the lobsters: In a large saucepan, combine the salt, vinegar, and enough water to cover the lobsters and bring the water to a boil. Add the lobsters and cook for approximately 7 to 10 minutes; the lobsters should be slightly undercooked. When cool enough to handle, remove lobster meat and dice it into $^1/_2$-inch pieces. Reserve the shells and legs for garnishing the plates.

3. Cook the scallops: In a large saucepan, heat the olive oil until very hot. Add sliced scallops and brown lightly, approximately 2 minutes. Add the

lobster meat and sauté, stirring, until the mixture turns orange, about 5 minutes. Remove the scallops to the bowl of potato mixture. Strain the liquid in the pan and reserve it for making lobster bisque or for another purpose.

4. Add the lobster to the scallop and potato mixture. Incorporate the chopped herbs. With a rubber spatula, break up the potatoes a little. Mix well. Season with salt and pepper to taste.

5. Make the rosemary sauce: In a saucepan, melt 1 tablespoon butter, add shallots, and sauté until brown. Add veal stock and cook over medium heat until reduced by one-quarter. Strain the sauce into a bowl, add the rosemary sprig, infuse for 5 minutes, and then remove the rosemary. Whisk in the butter and season with the pepper. Reheat the sauce in a saucepan over low heat just prior to serving.

6. Make the *provençale*: Preheat the oven to 250 degrees F. Make an **X** on the bottom of each tomato. Blanch the tomatoes in a large pot of boiling water for a few seconds. Remove with a slotted spoon. Remove the skin and seeds and cut the tomatoes into chunks. Heat 1 tablespoon olive oil in a large saucepan and sauté shallots and garlic until shallots are translucent. Add the tomato chunks, bay leaves, and thyme. Cover with parchment, then bake for 1/2 hour in a slow oven. When finished, remove the bay leaves and process with basil leaves in a food processor for a few seconds.

7. To serve, place a 3-inch metal ring on each dinner plate. Fill the ring three-quarters full with the potato-lobster mixture and flatten with a large wooden spoon. Top each serving with approximately 1 tablespoon of the *provençale*, or enough to cover. Level with a metal spatula. Place plates on a cookie sheet in a warm oven for a few minutes. Remove the rings. Garnish each timbale with a basil leaf and drizzle the plate with the rosemary sauce.

N O T E :   If a metal ring is unavailable, cut out the top and bottom of a clean tunafish can and use the sides as a mold.

O P T I O N A L :   Prior to serving, heat the olive oil in a sauté pan over medium heat and sauté the shrimp and scallops until lightly browned. Discard any excess oil, whisk in the butter, and season with salt and pepper to taste. Arrange the shrimps and scallops, alternating them, over the rosemary sauce. Each serving should have at least 2 shrimp and 2 scallops.

S E R V E S 6

13

This smoked salmon bouquet is the perfect appetizer for the healthy sensualist. Kalamansi, a fruit similar to a lime that combines the tastes of orange and lime, sensuously accents the raw salmon. Originated in Thailand, kalamansi is now cultivated in Florida.

SMOKED SALMON BOUQUET WITH CAVIAR

LESPINASSE

4 tablespoons finely chopped celery

salt and white pepper to taste

juice of 1 kalamansi (if unavailable, substitute fresh lime juice)

1 tablespoon olive oil

1/4 teaspoon sugar

2 ounces smoked salmon

15 pink peppercorns, finely chopped

12 endive leaves

1/2 pound mesclun (mixed greens) or frisée

1 teaspoon caviar

2 branches chervil

4 edible flowers, such as chive or thyme, if in season

1/2 small loaf pumpernickel bread, crust only, cut into strips

2 dried red peppers, seeds removed, finely chopped into flakes

1. In a bowl, season the celery with salt and pepper to taste, all but 1 tablespoon of the *kalamansi* juice, olive oil, and sugar.

2. Cut the salmon into 1/2-ounce pieces (2 1/2 inches long) and place each piece between 2 sheets of plastic wrap. Pound the salmon with the flat side of a knife blade.

3. Line four 2- × 1-inch round molds with a 4-inch-long piece of plastic wrap. Gently center each salmon piece in a mold. Divide the celery mixture among the molds and then fold the salmon pieces toward the center overlapping one another. Cover with plastic wrap and press to secure the mold.

4. Crush pink peppercorns through a sieve to remove the pods. Reserve.

5. To serve, place 3 leaves of endive on each plate, 1 inch away from each other and with the tips pointing outward like a flower. Portion the salad greens in the middle of each plate. Unwrap the salmon and unmold, inverting in the center of each plate; spoon a small amount of caviar on top. Arrange a sprig of chervil on each endive leaf.

6. Place 1 petal of an edible flower on top of the caviar and drizzle with the remaining *kalamansi* juice. Place 5 pumpernickel-crust juliennes around each plate. Sprinkle reserved pink peppercorns and red pepper flakes around the plate for decoration.

HINT FROM THE CHEF: Garden and fresh-cut flowers cannot be used in cooking as they may contain toxic pesticides that can be harmful.

SERVES 4

SALMON CARPACCIO WITH GREEN SAUCE

IL NIDO

1 pound fresh salmon filet, $^1/_4$ pound per person, cut into 2-inch-wide filets

corn oil

1 cup Italian parsley, stemmed

3 gherkins

$^1/_2$ large white onion, peeled

$^1/_4$ cup extra-virgin olive oil

salt and freshly ground black pepper to taste

juice of $^1/_2$ lemon

4 pieces toasted white bread, cut into quarters

GARNISH
1 lemon, thinly sliced

This velvety, paper-thin raw salmon filet typifies the subtlety of northern Italian cuisine. The savory green sauce provides an elegant, refreshing coating.

1. Using a fish tweezer, carefully remove the salmon bones. Trim off the fat and the brown undersides. With an iron pounder, pound the salmon paper-thin between sheets of wax paper that have been brushed with corn oil.

2. In a food processor, chop the parsley, gherkins, and onion for 5 minutes, until a smooth purée forms. Add the olive oil and lemon juice, salt and pepper to taste, and process for 30 seconds. If you are not using the sauce immediately, pour it into an airtight container and refrigerate.

3. When ready to serve, remove the top sheet of wax paper and, grasping the bottom sheet of wax paper, place the salmon on a dinner plate with the wax paper facing up. Gently remove the wax paper. Spoon the green sauce onto the salmon and spread gently, using the back of a spoon. Serve with crustless white-bread toast points. Garnish with lemon slices.

SERVES 4

An exotic and dazzling mélange of sautéed shrimp and cabbage is sandwiched between diaphanous sheets of pasta with a leaf of shiso (Japanese beefsteak mint) peeking through the top layer. This diverse dish creatively combines classic French cooking technique, Italian lasagna, American herb oils, herbal fragrances, and Oriental seasonings.

Proprietor André Jammet descends from a family with a long history of restaurant ownership that dates back to the grand Paris hotel, The Bristol. The Jammets' restaurant, La Caravelle, remains one of New York's culinary gems.

SHRIMP AND SCALLOP LASAGNA WITH SALMON ROE

LA CARAVELLE

PASTA (makes sixteen 4-inch rounds or use round dumpling skins)

1 egg yolk

$^1/_4$ cup salted soda water

2 cups all-purpose flour

$^1/_2$ teaspoon salt

BEURRE BLANC

$^1/_4$ cup dry white wine

1 teaspoon white wine vinegar

1 tablespoon chopped shallots

1 teaspoon heavy cream

10 tablespoons cold sweet butter, cut into bits

salt and freshly ground white pepper to taste

1 tablespoon sweet butter

2 cups julienned cabbage

2 cups julienned leeks

1 teaspoon finely chopped ginger

4 tablespoons heavy cream

2 tablespoons vegetable oil

24 bay scallops

1 teaspoon sweet butter

12 large shrimp, shelled and deveined

EGG WASH

1 egg yolk

2 tablespoons water

4 leaves Japanese beefsteak mint (shiso)

4 teaspoons Chili Oil (page 198)

4 teaspoons Basil Oil (page 198)

GARNISH

4 teaspoons flying fish roe (miniature salmon roe)

1. Make the pasta: Mix together the egg yolk and soda water. Add the egg yolk mixture to the flour and salt, and with your hands form the dough into a ball. Wrap in plastic wrap and refrigerate for 6 hours. Remove the plastic wrap and flatten the dough with a rolling pin or use a pasta machine. Roll out the pasta dough very thin on a lightly floured surface and cut it into sixteen 4-inch rounds using a 4-inch metal ring. Discard the remaining dough.

2. Bring 1 quart of salted water to a boil.

3. Make the *beurre blanc*: In a nonreactive saucepan, cook the wine, vinegar, and shallots, and reduce until almost dry. Add the cream to moisten, then whisk in well the cold butter bits. Season with salt and pepper to taste. Keep warm in a *bain-marie*.

4. Melt 1 tablespoon of butter in a large saucepan over low heat and add the cabbage, leeks, and ginger, cooking slowly and stirring constantly until the vegetables soften, at least ¹/₂ hour. Add the heavy cream to moisten and stir to combine.

5. In a sauté pan, heat 1 tablespoon of the oil until smoking-hot and sauté the scallops until nicely colored. Add to the cabbage mixture.

6. Heat the remaining tablespoon of oil and the remaining butter until hot. Sauté the shrimp for 2 to 3 minutes.

7. Make the egg wash: Lightly beat the egg yolk and the water.

8. Cook the pasta for 1 minute in the rapidly boiling water. Remove it with a large slotted metal spoon.

9. Arrange 2 pasta rounds next to one another on the work surface. Brush the sides facing you with the egg wash. Place 1 *shiso* leaf in the center of one round, and cover that round with the second round wash side down, pressing together gently. Make 3 more rounds in the same manner.

10. To serve, put a 3-inch metal ring in the center of each dinner plate and place a pasta round in it. Spoon 2 tablespoons of the cabbage-scallop mixture in the middle of the ring. Top with a pasta round and cover it with several shrimp. Top with a *shiso* leaf double pasta round. Remove the ring. Spoon the warm *beurre blanc* around the pasta, to the rim of the plate, decorating the plate like an abstract painting. Arrange miniature salmon roe in a circle around the inner rim of the plate. Drizzle the chili and basil oils over the top layer of the pasta. Following the same procedure, make 3 more servings with the remaining ingredients.

SERVES 4

Muglai Indian cuisine, originated by a sixteenth-century Mogul emperor, features grilling and aromatic sauces. This spicy grilled chicken, tenderized with yogurt and seasoned with a fiery mint chutney, is the perfect finger food for a party.

GREEN CHICKEN WINGS

AKBAR

3 pounds chicken wings

coarse salt to taste

¹/₄ cup fresh lemon juice

2 tablespoons nut or corn oil

1 CUP GREEN CHUTNEY

1 green bell pepper, seeded

1 ripe medium tomato, seeded

1 cup mint leaves, stems removed

¹/₂ cup fresh coriander leaves

4 fresh green chilies, stalks removed

1 teaspoon minced garlic

1 teaspoon minced ginger

¹/₃ cup low-fat plain yogurt

1 tablespoon ground cumin

1 Spanish onion, peeled and sliced into rings

1 teaspoon chat masala (*see Hints from the Chef*)

GARNISH

¹/₂ cup chopped fresh coriander

1 lemon, cut into wedges

1. Rub the chicken pieces with salt and sprinkle with lemon juice and oil. Set aside for 30 minutes.

2. Make the green chutney: In a food processor, purée the bell pepper, tomato, mint and coriander leaves until smooth. Add the chilies, process, and then place in a small bowl.

3. Add the garlic and ginger to the food processor and purée into a paste. Mix with the 1 cup green chutney, low-fat yogurt, cumin, and salt to taste. Pour marinade over the chicken and marinate for 2 hours in the refrigerator. Bring the chicken to room temperature before grilling.

4. Preheat a lightly oiled grill or the oven to 375 degrees F. Grill the chicken until tender, approximately 8 to 10 minutes, or bake in the oven for 15 to 20 minutes, leaving some of the marinade adhering to the chicken.

5. To serve, arrange the onion rings on a platter and sprinkle with *chat masala*. Then place the chicken on top and garnish with chopped coriander and lemon wedges.

HINTS FROM THE CHEF: You can increase the quantity of the fresh chilies depending on the desired hotness. *Chat masala* can be found in Indian grocery stores. If unavailable, substitute equal amounts of ground cumin, paprika, ground coriander, crushed or ground red chili powder, and ground fenugreek. Fenugreek is a flat yellow or orange seed with a slightly bitter taste.

SERVES 6

SALMON TARTARE WITH OYSTERS

AQUAVIT

1 egg yolk

1/2 teaspoon Dijon mustard

3 tablespoons olive oil

1 tablespoon capers

1 tablespoon minced, fresh shallots

1 tablespoon chopped cornichons

1 teaspoon finely chopped sardines

12 ounces fresh Norwegian salmon, finely diced

4 large belon oysters, finely diced, with their liquid

1 tablespoon fresh lemon juice

pinch of salt

freshly ground white pepper to taste

GARNISH

4 tablespoons salmon caviar

This creation illustrates Aquavit's penchant for light and fresh ingredients. Although salmon tartare has many variations, the addition of oysters, the prized mollusk, provides a distinguished flavor.

Aquavit occupies an historic, elegant townhouse that once belonged to the Rockefellers. Its main dining room features an eight-story skylit space, colorful fabric kites, and dramatic waterfalls.

1. Place the egg yolk and mustard in a nonreactive bowl; beat in the oil slowly. Add the capers, shallots, cornichons, and sardines, and mix well. With a wooden spoon, fold in the salmon, oysters, oyster liquid, and lemon juice. Season with salt and freshly ground white pepper to taste.

2. Divide the tartare into six portions, placing an oval-shaped scoop on each of six appetizer-size plates. Cover each plate with plastic wrap and refrigerate for 1 hour.

3. To serve, garnish each serving with salmon caviar. Serve with toast points or crisp bread. Accompany with seasonal salad tossed with tart vinaigrette.

HINTS FROM THE CHEF: Norwegian salmon is recommended because its high fat content provides a subtler and more luxurious flavor than other salmons. Only the freshest fish can be used for this dish. Because sardines have their own natural salt, season the tartare with care. Follow the classic rule that oysters should be eaten only in those months that are spelled with an "r."

SERVES 6

Nigiri, *Japanese for the word "grasp," is the most popular type of sushi, made by shaping the freshest piece of fish on top of a small mound of rice. A smear of pungent wasabi adds a striking contrast to the smooth consistency of the rice and fish.*

Sushi chefs are culinary artists and spend two years training to prepare sushi rice. My training with sushi chef Massai Seki reinforced the need for staccato-like arm movements when cutting the rice to retain its moisture.

NIGIRI SUSHI

HATSUHANA

RICE

3 cups short-grain Japanese rice

3 cups water

$^1/_3$ cup rice vinegar

1 teaspoon sugar

1 teaspoon salt

4 jumbo shrimp, shelled and deveined

MARINADE

$^2/_3$ cup rice vinegar

2 teaspoons sugar

2 teaspoons salt

$^1/_4$ pound filet of tuna or fluke, or another fresh, sushi quality fish

EEL SUSHI

5 tablespoons Japanese soy sauce

2 tablespoons sugar

3 tablespoons mirin

$^1/_4$ pound water eel (available in the freezer section of Japanese markets)

1 piece of Nori seaweed, 4 by 7 inches, cut into $^1/_2$-inch strips

GARNISH

4 tablespoons pickled ginger

1 tablespoon wasabi or green horseradish paste

2 tablespoons Japanese soy sauce

1. Make the *sushi* rice: Rinse the rice with water several times until the water runs clear. Let the rice sit in a strainer for 30 minutes.

2. In an electric rice cooker, combine the rice and the 3 cups water. Cook for 20 minutes. Let the rice rest, covered, for 15 to 20 minutes. (If a rice cooker is unavailable, cook the rice in water until tender.)

3. Make the marinade: In a bowl, mix together the rice vinegar, sugar, and salt.

4. In a large, low-sided wooden bowl, sprinkle a few drops of the vinegar solution to dampen the center of the bowl. Add the rice, then pour the rest of the vinegar solution over it. With the back of a large wooden spoon or slightly rounded spatula dipped in water, cut the rice with quick diagonal motions. Cool a little with a hand fan (if available) and let the rice rest for 10 minutes. Then section by section, fold rice over and smooth again with the back of the spoon. Let the mixture sit for 2 minutes. Line a medium-size bowl with plastic wrap, leaving enough extra on the sides to fold them in to cover the bowl later. Then line the inside of the bowl with cheesecloth. Wet a large wooden spoon and with it remove the rice to the bowl. Cover the top of the bowl with the extra plastic wrap until ready to use.

5. Make the rice pieces: Wet one hand with some vinegar, then shape the rice with your fingertips into small rectangles approximately 2^1/$_2$ inches long and 1 inch thick. (If the rice sticks to your hands, wipe them with a wet towel or dip your hands in water.)

6. Make the shrimp *sushi*: Place long, thin toothpicks through the shrimp lengthwise to prevent curling during cooking. Cook the shrimp in rapidly boiling salted water for about 3 minutes. Drain and cut the shrimp lengthwise down the middle. Marinate in the vinegar marinade for 5 minutes. Place 1 opened shrimp in your left hand and with your right index finger smear ^{1}/$_4$ teaspoon *wasabi* down it; mold a rectangular rice piece to each shrimp.

7. Make the tuna *sushi*: Use a sharp knife to cut the tuna along the grain into 3- × 1-inch pieces, each ^{1}/$_4$ inch thick. Place each tuna piece in your left hand and with your right index finger smear ^{1}/$_4$ teaspoon *wasabi* down it; mold a rectangular rice piece to each piece of tuna.

8. Make the eel *sushi*: Begin by combining the soy sauce, sugar, and *mirin* in a small bowl. Thaw the frozen eel by dipping it in warm water for a few minutes to soften. Then warm in a toaster oven for several minutes until heated through and cut into 2- × 3-inch pieces. Take a piece of eel, place it on top and in the center of 1 tablespoon *sushi* rice, and wrap tightly with a ^{1}/$_2$-inch strip of seaweed. Brush the eel and seaweed with the *mirin* and soy sauce mixture.

9. Serve *sushi* immediately with the fish on top. Garnish the tray with pickled ginger, *wasabi*, and soy sauce.

SERVES 4

Innovative chef David Waltuck is renowned for his unusual combinations of ingredients. His keen appreciation of flowers is evident in these tender zucchini blossoms filled with shellfish and presented in a creamy tomato sauce scented with fresh mint.

STEAMED ZUCCHINI BLOSSOMS FILLED WITH SHRIMP AND LOBSTER

CHANTERELLE

COURT BOUILLON

1 gallon water

12 peppercorns

1 large onion, peeled and chopped

3 bay leaves

1 cup dry white wine

2 tablespoons kosher salt

2 cups chopped carrots

juice of 1 lemon

1 live 1-pound lobster

12 large zucchini blossoms (with baby zucchini attached)

FILLING

1/2 pound fresh shrimp, shelled and deveined

1 egg white

kosher salt

1/4 cup heavy cream, chilled (not ultra-pasteurized)

1/4 teaspoon finely chopped garlic

1 teaspoon brandy

freshly ground black pepper to taste

pinch of cayenne pepper

FISH SAUCE

1 tablespoon sweet butter

1 carrot, unpeeled and coarsely chopped

1 small onion, unpeeled and coarsely chopped

1 head of garlic, unpeeled and coarsely chopped

1/4 cup dry white wine

1 cup Fish Stock (page 204)

1 cup canned Italian tomatoes, crushed

1 large bunch mint (2 to 3 ounces), coarsely chopped, stems included

1 cup heavy cream (not ultra-pasteurized)

juice of 1/2 lemon

GARNISH

2 tablespoons mint chiffonnade (cut into thin strips)

4 mint sprigs

1. Make the *court bouillon*: Fill a large pot with 1 gallon of water and add the peppercorns, onion, bay leaves, wine, salt, carrots, and lemon juice. Bring the mixture to a boil.

2. Add the lobster and simmer it for 5 minutes. Remove the lobster from the pot, let cool, take off the shell, and finely chop the meat.

3. Remove the pistils from the insides of the blossoms. If baby zucchini are attached to the flowers, make 3 or 4 lengthwise slices three-quarters of the way up each zucchini.

4. Make the filling: Place the shrimp, egg white, and a pinch of salt in a food processor and purée. Add the chilled cream and process until the mixture reaches the consistency of a paste. Place the mixture in a bowl. Add the lobster meat, garlic, and brandy and season with salt, black pepper, and cayenne. Mix well with a rubber spatula.

5. Add the filling to a pastry bag and generously pipe it into the zucchini blossoms. Twist the end of each blossom to seal.

6. Steam the flowers in a bamboo steamer over boiling water in a saucepan for approximately 5 minutes, or until the filling feels firm and cooked. If zucchini are not attached to the blossoms, steam them separately by fanning them out in the steamer.

7. Make the sauce: Melt the butter in a large saucepan, add the carrot, onion, and garlic, cover, and sweat over low heat until translucent. Add the wine and reduce until almost evaporated. Add the fish stock, tomatoes, and mint, bring to a boil, then simmer over low heat for 30 minutes. Strain the liquid through a fine sieve or *chinois* into a clean pan, pressing down on the solids to extract all of the juices, and making sure not to push the vegetables through.

8. Add the cream to the liquid, bring to a boil, and reduce until slightly thickened, or until it lightly coats the back of a wooden spoon. Add lemon juice, and season with salt and black pepper to taste.

9. To serve, spoon 4 tablespoons of sauce onto each dinner plate, sprinkle with mint, and arrange 3 zucchini blossoms on the sauce so that the leaves turn outward and touch each other in the center. Garnish with a mint sprig in the center of the plate where the zucchini blossoms meet.

SERVES 4

VEGETABLE TERRINE WITH HERBES DE PROVENCE

This vegetable terrine exemplifies Chef Debra Ponzek's love for the bold seasonings and flavors of Provence. Savory, thyme, and oregano are plentiful in the south of France and are typically used in Provençale cooking. Drizzled with roasted red pepper oil, this dish is as magnificent to the eye as it is to the taste.

MONTRACHET

2 zucchini

2 yellow squash

1 small eggplant, peeled

salt and freshly ground white pepper to taste

2 tablespoons plus 1 cup olive oil

1 large onion, peeled and thinly sliced

1¹/₂ teaspoons chopped fresh thyme

6 red bell peppers, roasted, peeled, seeded, and halved

12 ounces goat cheese (1 log plus 1 ounce), at room temperature

HERBES DE PROVENCE

a mixture of 2 teaspoons each of dried thyme, parsley, and savory

1. Preheat the broiler. Thinly slice the zucchini and squash horizontally and the eggplant vertically into ¹/₈-inch slices, either by hand or, preferably, with a *mandoline*. Arrange the slices of each vegetable on a separate baking sheet so that they do not overlap. Season with salt and pepper to taste. Broil for 2 to 3 minutes. Reserve.

2. Heat 2 tablespoons olive oil in a saucepan and add the onion, salt and pepper, and the fresh thyme. Sauté until the onion is translucent. Allow to cool.

3. In a 10- ✕ 4-inch terrine or shallow pan, layer the eggplant until it is about ¹/₂ inch deep on the bottom of the terrine. Cut the pieces to fit so that they lay flat. Lay the halves of 4 of the roasted red peppers evenly over the eggplant. Place the goat cheese on top of the peppers, spreading the cheese *as evenly as possible* and filling in any gaps in the layers. Add the yellow squash, arranging the slices in as even a layer as possible. Then add the sautéed onion, spreading it evenly over the squash. Finish the terrine with a layer of zucchini. Cover with plastic wrap.

4. Cut a piece of cardboard the same size as the terrine mold, put it over the plastic wrap, and place a 2-pound weight on top of it. Let the terrine sit overnight in the refrigerator.

5. Make the roasted red pepper oil: In a food processor, purée the remaining 2 roasted peppers until smooth. Slowly drizzle in 1 cup olive oil and process until smooth. Season with salt and pepper to taste. Strain the oil through a fine-mesh sieve into an air-tight container and refrigerate until ready to use.

6. Turn the mold upside down and remove the mold from the terrine. Preferably using an electric knife, slice the terrine into 1-inch-thick pieces. Place the slices on pieces of aluminum foil a little larger than the slice, and prior to serving heat them until warm in a 350 degree F. oven. Place each slice on a large dinner plate, sprinkle with *herbes de Provence,* and drizzle with roasted red pepper oil.

HINT FROM THE CHEF: It is important that the mold be covered with plastic wrap and ladened with a weight equal to that of a brick. The mold must be removed when cold.

SERVES 10

SOUPS

*Savored since Roman times, the
artichoke, a fleshy Mediterranean
thistle, remains a delicacy. This
creamless, tasty artichoke soup,
thickened with potato, exemplifies
David Burke's light and elegant
cuisine.*

ARTICHOKE SOUP WITH BAY SCALLOPS

PARK AVENUE CAFE

8 tablespoons sweet butter

2 cups chopped leeks (white part only)

2 potatoes, peeled and chopped

8 cups Light Chicken Stock (page 203)

3 medium artichokes, stems removed

coarse or kosher salt and freshly ground
 white pepper to taste

18 bay scallops

$^1/_2$ cup chopped chives

1. Heat the butter in a sauté pan and sauté the leeks and potatoes for 10 minutes. Reserve.

2. Make the artichoke stock: In a large soup pot over high heat, bring the chicken stock and artichokes to a boil. Reduce to a simmer and cook for 35 minutes. Using a slotted spoon, remove the artichokes from the stock and place under running water. Remove the artichoke leaves and return them to the stock. Set the artichokes aside. Bring the stock to a simmer and cook an additional 15 minutes. Strain the stock and discard the leaves. Return the stock to the pot.

3. Remove the chokes from the artichoke bottoms and dice the bottoms.

4. Add the sautéed leeks and potatoes to the artichoke stock and simmer for 25 minutes, or until the potatoes are cooked. Season to taste with the salt and pepper. Ladle the soup into a food processor and purée. Return the soup to the pot, straining if necessary.

5. Bring the soup to a simmer, add the diced artichoke bottoms and scallops, and cook for 2 to 3 minutes. Stir in the chives. Remove the scallops from the soup with a slotted spoon and thread 3 each onto 6 bamboo skewers. Ladle the soup into soup plates and lay a bamboo skewer across each.

SERVES 6

WILD MUSHROOM SOUP

FELIDIA

8 dried porcini mushrooms, about 3
   ounces, coarsely chopped
10 tablespoons olive oil
1 medium onion, peeled and chopped
2 tablespoons chopped pancetta (Italian
   bacon) or prosciutto, optional
2 medium potatoes, peeled and diced
2 whole medium carrots, peeled and
   chopped
1 large shallot, peeled and chopped
10 cups Light Chicken Stock (page
   203)

$^1/_2$ teaspoon salt
2 pounds fresh wild mushrooms, cleaned
   and sliced
freshly ground black pepper to taste

GARNISH
$^1/_4$ cup finely chopped Italian parsley
4 tablespoons freshly grated Parmesan
   cheese

*This earthy soup is the best wild
mushroom soup I have ever tasted.
Savory porcini and fresh wild
mushrooms lend a pungent and
intoxicating aroma, while the
vegetables provide the soup's
density.*

1. Soak the *porcini* in 1$^1/_2$ cups warm water for approximately 20 minutes,
until softened. Remove the mushrooms and strain all but the last 2 teaspoons
of the soaking liquid, leaving any sediment behind. Reserve the liquid.

2. In a 5-quart soup pot, heat 5 tablespoons olive oil and sauté the onion and
pancetta over medium heat until crispy. Add the potatoes, carrots, and shallot
and cook for 2 minutes, stirring constantly.

3. Add the stock, drained *porcini*, and reserved mushroom liquid. Season with
salt and bring to a boil. Reduce the heat and simmer over low heat for
approximately 10 minutes.

4. Heat the remaining 5 tablespoons of oil in a saucepan. Add the fresh wild
mushrooms and sauté for 7 minutes in batches over medium high heat until
the water evaporates. Transfer the mushrooms to the soup pot and continue
simmering for 30 minutes, skimming occasionally. Season with pepper to
taste.

5. To serve, garnish the soup with the parsley and Parmesan cheese.

SERVES 8

Dotted with flaky morsels of crabmeat and infused with the flavors of sherry and fresh fennel, this bisque makes an elegant presentation for a holiday meal or any special occasion. Chef Waldy Malouf favors long-cooked soups, and here he transforms classic lobster bisque into a lighter, yet intensely flavorful version that celebrates the local ingredients of the Northeast seaboard.

CRAB AND SCALLOP BISQUE

HUDSON RIVER CLUB

3 tablespoons Clarified Butter (page 196)

1 medium Spanish onion, peeled and sliced

1 large carrot, peeled and sliced

2 stalks celery, sliced

1 leek, white part only, cleaned and sliced

1 fennel bulb, thinly sliced

$^1/_3$ cup tomato paste

$^1/_3$ cup unconverted rice

$^1/_4$ cup brandy

$^1/_4$ cup sherry

4 cups Fish Stock (page 204)

4 cups Light Chicken Stock (page 203)

herb sachet (tied together in a double layer of cheesecloth):

  1 teaspoon black peppercorns

  2 bay leaves

  2 garlic cloves, unpeeled and smashed

  2 sprigs thyme

  4 sprigs tarragon, with stems, chopped

9 medium hard-shell Long Island crabs, cleaned, chopped, and halved

$^1/_4$ pound Long Island bay scallops

4 tablespoons sweet butter, at room temperature

2 tablespoons flour

$^1/_2$ cup heavy cream

coarse salt and freshly ground black pepper to taste

GARNISH
4 tablespoons chopped tarragon leaves

1. In a heavy 6-quart soup pot, heat the clarified butter over medium heat, and sauté the onion, carrot, celery, leek, and fennel until translucent, approximately 10 to 15 minutes, stirring frequently. Add the tomato paste and stir for a few minutes. Add the rice and stir.

2. Over low heat, add the brandy and sherry, increase the heat and stir constantly until the liquid almost evaporates. Add the fish and chicken stocks and the herb sachet, bring the mixture to a boil, and simmer for 45 minutes. Strain the soup through a *chinois* or strainer into a bowl, pressing on the solids to extract as much liquid as possible.

3. Rinse out the pot and return the soup to it. Bring the soup to a boil, add the crabs, and return the soup to a boil. Reduce the heat and simmer for 30 minutes. Stir the crabs 2 or 3 times to ensure even cooking. Strain the soup. Spread the crabs on a large flat surface. Using a nutcracker, a nutpick, and your fingers, remove the meat and the roe from the crabs and reserve.

4. In a small saucepan, bring 1 cup of soup to a boil. Reduce the heat and gently poach the scallops in the soup for 3 or 4 minutes. Strain the scallop-soup mixture into the rest of the soup, reserving the scallops.

5. Using a wooden spoon or your hands, work the butter and flour together for approximately 5 minutes to form a *beurre-manié*. Bring the soup to a boil, whisk in the *beurre-manié*, and simmer the soup for several minutes. Whisk in the cream, bring the soup to a boil, and simmer for an additional 5 minutes. Stir in the reserved scallops, the crabmeat, and the roe. Season with salt and pepper to taste.

6. To serve, spoon out scallops and crabmeat from the soup, dividing evenly among 8 warmed bowls. Spoon in the soup. Garnish with a generous pinch of chopped tarragon.

SERVES 8

FISH SOUP WITH SAFFRON

HARRY CIPRIANI

8 cups Fish Stock (page 204)

$^1/_8$ teaspoon powdered saffron (or $^1/_4$ teaspoon saffron threads)

7 tablespoons olive oil

2 stalks celery, julienned

2 medium onions, peeled and julienned

1 carrot, peeled and julienned

2 bay leaves

1 medium tomato, peeled, cored, seeded, and julienned

$^1/_4$ cup flour plus extra for dredging

1 cup dry white wine

$^1/_8$ teaspoon cayenne pepper (dried ground red hot pepper)

salt and freshly ground white pepper to taste

$^1/_2$ pound boneless skinless sea bass or red snapper, cut into $^1/_2$-inch cubes

$^1/_2$ pound boneless halibut or swordfish (or any other white fish), cut into $^1/_2$-inch cubes

$^1/_2$ pound medium shrimp, shelled and halved

3 tablespoons brandy

2 anchovy filets, chopped

1 fresh sprig rosemary, broken

1 fresh sprig thyme, broken

3 sprigs flat-leaf parsley, chopped

1 garlic clove, peeled

GARNISH
3 flat-leaf parsley leaves, finely chopped

1. In a medium saucepan, heat the fish stock and in it dissolve the powdered saffron. If using threads, add them little by little.

2. In a soup pot, heat 2 tablespoons of the oil over medium heat. Add the celery, onions, and carrot and sauté, stirring frequently, for approximately 5 minutes, or until the vegetables soften. Add the bay leaves and the tomato and cook for another minute. Sprinkle the $^1/_4$ cup flour over the vegetables and cook for 2 minutes, stirring constantly to prevent lumps. Add the wine, stirring thoroughly until the mixture boils. Season with cayenne pepper and salt and white pepper to taste.

3. Add the fish stock to the vegetable mixture and bring the mixture to a boil over medium heat, skimming the top periodically. Simmer, partially covered, for 20 minutes.

4. Season the fish and shrimp with salt and pepper. Lightly flour the fish and shrimp and shake off the excess. In a large sauté pan, heat 2 tablespoons of the oil and brown the fish and shrimp on both sides—in batches, if necessary—tossing for approximately 2 to 3 minutes. Drain off excess oil.

5. Off the heat, flame the fish and shrimp by adding the brandy and swirl the pan over high heat until the flames extinguish. Add the mixture to the soup pot.

6. In a saucepan, make an aromatic oil by combining the remaining 3 tablespoons oil, the anchovies, rosemary, thyme, parsley, and garlic over medium heat, stirring constantly for 2 or 3 minutes. Strain out the herbs and garlic, pour only the oil into the soup, and stir well. Adjust the seasonings. Garnish with chopped parsley. Serve immediately.

HINTS FROM THE CHEF: Be careful to pour the brandy over the fish and shrimp off the heat since it will flame up. The pan must be returned to the stove immediately after that so that the brandy can be absorbed into the fish. If you chop the parsley in advance, wring out the water in a cloth towel.

SERVES 6

This colorful cold vegetable soup, inspired by France's world-renowned chef Roger Vergé, suits the Old World grandeur of the Edwardian Room. The ruby-colored room of the historic Plaza Hotel has a dream-like atmosphere, and with its views of Central Park and horse-drawn carriages, is a site unrivaled in New York City.

This magnificent soup is easy to prepare and versatile in that other vegetables may be substituted. For instance, use artichoke hearts instead of asparagus or make a soup of red, green, and yellow peppers instead of this four vegetable combination.

FOUR VEGETABLE SOUP

EDWARDIAN ROOM AT THE PLAZA

TOMATO SOUP
8 medium, ripe red tomatoes, peeled, seeded, and chopped
4 garlic cloves, peeled and mashed
$1/2$ cup heavy cream
salt and freshly ground white pepper to taste

RED PEPPER SOUP
1 pound red bell peppers, seeded and diced
$3/4$ cup water
salt and pinch of freshly ground white pepper
pinch of sugar
heavy cream to taste
Tabasco to taste

ASPARAGUS SOUP
1 pound asparagus, tips only
$6^{1}/2$ ounces spinach leaves, well cleaned and stems removed
heavy cream to taste
salt and freshly ground white pepper to taste
pinch of sugar

TURNIP SOUP
1 pound turnips, peeled
heavy cream to taste
4 or 5 saffron threads
salt and freshly ground white pepper to taste

GARNISH
4 tablespoons Crème Fraîche (page 196) or heavy cream, optional
2 tablespoons chopped chives or chervil

1. Make the tomato soup: Combine the tomatoes and garlic in a saucepan, whisk in the cream, and season with salt and white pepper to taste. Reduce the mixture over low heat until the tomatoes soften, approximately 20 minutes. In a blender or food processor, purée the mixture. Press through a fine sieve or *chinois* into a bowl and cover with plastic wrap. Refrigerate.

2. Make the red pepper soup: Combine the red peppers and water in a saucepan. Season with salt, white pepper, and sugar, cover, and cook over low heat until the peppers are soft. In a blender, purée the mixture then pass through a fine sieve or *chinois* into a bowl. Cover and refrigerate for 2 to 3 hours. When ready to serve, whisk in the cream, tablespoon by tablespoon, until the soup reaches the desired consistency. Season with Tabasco to taste.

3. Make the asparagus soup: Cook the asparagus in boiling salted water for 2 to 3 minutes, adding the spinach just before the asparagus are tender. Carefully remove the asparagus and spinach with a slotted spoon and place in a strainer. Plunge the asparagus into ice water for 2 to 3 minutes to fix the color. Drain well for approximately 5 minutes so that all the water drains off. Purée the asparagus and spinach in a blender for at least 2 minutes. Strain the purée through a fine sieve or *chinois* into a bowl and add the cream, tablespoon by tablespoon, until the mixture reaches the desired consistency. Season with salt, pepper, and sugar.

4. Make the turnip soup: In a large saucepan, bring 3 to 4 cups salted water to a boil, add the turnips, and cook until tender. Place the turnips in a *chinois* or strainer for 4 to 5 minutes, until all the water has drained. Purée the turnips in a food processor. Strain the purée through a fine sieve or *chinois* into a bowl, cover, and refrigerate for 2 to 3 hours. When ready to serve, add cream, little by little, until the soup reaches the desired consistency. Add the saffron and season with salt and freshly ground white pepper to taste. Cover with plastic wrap and chill for 2 to 3 hours.

5. To serve, ladle the tomato, asparagus, and turnip soups into the three sections of each soup bowl, carefully keeping them separate. Pour red pepper soup into the center. Garnish with a dollop of *crème fraîche* and make a design in the cream with a knife. Top with chives or chervil, or a combination of both.

HINTS FROM THE CHEF: The turnip soup requires more cream than either the bell pepper or tomato soup, where a small amount will suffice. To make a lighter version of Four Vegetable Soup, replace the heavy cream with an equal amount of Light Chicken Stock (page 203).

SERVES 4

This sour-spicy variation on classic mushroom broth is light and flavorful. Unlike Chinese hot-and-sour soup with thickener, all the flavors are heightened here by the essence of this exotic broth, which tantalizes the taste buds. Lemongrass, in particular, infuses the soup with an evanescent scent.

Trained in Switzerland by world-class chef Freddy Girardet, Chef Gray Kunz journeyed to Hong Kong and Thailand and has been fascinated ever since by Southeast Asian flavors.

SOUR-SPICY BROTH OF HON SHIMEJI MUSHROOMS

LESPINASSE

MUSHROOM BROTH
1/2 cup shiitake or chanterelle mushrooms, sliced, stems and trimmings reserved
3 tablespoons corn oil
sea salt to taste
4 tablespoons finely chopped ginger
3 tablespoons chopped lemongrass
1 tablespoon chopped garlic
2 tablespoons minced shallots
4 tablespoons tarragon vinegar
2 cups Vegetable Stock (page 208)
1 tablespoon sugar

3 tablespoons butter

1/4 cup hon shimeji mushrooms or sliced shiitake mushrooms
4 mint leaves chiffonnade (cut into thin shreds)
1 tomato, skinned, seeded, and diced
2 tablespoons destemmed watercress leaves
1 lotus root, very thinly sliced (24 slices)
1/2 cup fresh pineapple juice
1/2 teaspoon tamarind paste, optional
pinch of cayenne pepper
4 tablespoons chives, greens only

GARNISH
4 blades lemongrass

1. Preheat the oven to 500 degrees F.

2. Make the mushroom broth: In an ovenproof skillet, sear the mushroom trimmings and stems in corn oil. Add salt, 3 tablespoons chopped ginger, 2 tablespoons lemongrass, 1 tablespoon garlic, 1 tablespoon shallot, and shiitake or chanterelle mushrooms. Caramelize in the oven for approximately 7 minutes. Return to the stove, add the tarragon vinegar, and deglaze over medium heat. Add the vegetable stock and simmer for 20 minutes. Pass through a chinois into a saucepan. Adjust with vinegar, salt, and sugar, if necessary. Reserve.

3. In a saucepan, sweat the remaining shallots in 2 tablespoons of the butter for approximately 2 minutes. Add the hon shimeji mushrooms, salt, remaining ginger, and remaining lemongrass and cook over medium heat. Add a pinch of sugar, the shredded mint, and 1 1/2 cups of the mushroom broth. Add the diced tomato, watercress leaves, lotus root slices, pineapple juice, tamarind paste, and cayenne pepper and bring to a boil. Adjust the seasoning by adding salt, pepper, and vinegar, if necessary. Finish by whisking in the remaining butter and the chive greens.

4. Garnish each serving with a blade of lemongrass.

NOTE: To extract the juice from a pineapple, juice half a peeled and cored pineapple in an electric juicer. If a juicer is not available, cook the pineapple in a saucepan over medium heat for ½ hour and strain off the juice.

SERVES 4

This flavorful potato and leek bouillon illustrates the use of French cooking techniques in the new American cuisine. Culinary dexterity is needed to create these uncommonly light goat cheese gnocchi.

POTATO AND LEEK BOUILLON WITH THYME GOAT CHEESE GNOCCHI

PRIX FIXE

POTATO AND LEEK
    BOUILLON
1/4 cup extra-virgin olive oil
3 cups leeks, well-rinsed and cut into
    1-inch thick pieces
1 cup onion chunks
2 garlic cloves, peeled and crushed
1 cup chopped stalk celery
1 3/4 pounds Yukon gold potatoes, peeled
    and sliced 1/4 inch thick
10 cups Light Chicken Stock (page
    203) or water
bouquet garni: 1 bay leaf and 1 sprig
    fresh thyme tied securely together with
    cotton twine
2 tablespoons sea salt
freshly ground white pepper to taste

THYME GOAT CHEESE
    GNOCCHI
1 1/4 pounds Yukon gold potatoes, peeled
    and cut into large pieces
2 tablespoons kosher salt
1/3 plus 1/4 cup all-purpose flour, sifted
1/3 cup aged goat cheese, grated
1 teaspoon chopped fresh thyme
cayenne pepper and white pepper to taste
2 large egg yolks

GARNISH
3 medium leeks, well washed and
    julienned
1 cup canola or vegetable oil
salt to taste
6 tablespoons finely chopped chives
3 teaspoons grated goat cheese

1. Make the potato and leek bouillon: In a medium stockpot, heat the olive oil and add the leeks, onion, garlic, and celery. Cover and sweat over medium heat for 12 minutes, until softened and colorless, stirring occasionally. Add the potatoes, chicken stock, and bouquet garni. Skim off the starch from the potatoes until the liquid boils, then simmer the soup for 40 minutes, or until the potatoes are tender. Strain through a *chinois* into a pan to extract the liquid and add the sea salt and pepper to taste.

2. Make the thyme and goat cheese *gnocchi*: Preheat the oven to 325 degrees F. Place the potatoes in a medium stockpot, cover with cold water, and add the salt. Simmer until the potatoes are tender, about 20 minutes. Drain the potatoes, place them on a baking pan, and dry them in the oven for about 12 minutes. Pass them through a food mill. (It is advisable to prepare these in advance so that the potatoes are less glutinous and dry well.) In a large bowl, combine the potatoes, 1/3 cup sifted flour, goat cheese, thyme, 1 tablespoon salt, and cayenne and white peppers. Gently stir in the egg yolks with a

wooden spoon. Mix by hand and knead like dough. Transfer to a pastry bag without a tip. Pipe out onto a lightly floured work surface in 12-inch-long pieces; cut the logs on the diagonal into thirty 1-inch-long pieces. Alternatively, roll the dough by hand into 1-inch pieces. Lightly flour the *gnocchi*, then roll, pressing each one with the back of a fork to create a nice design.

3. Bring a pot of salted water to a boil, add the *gnocchi*, and poach them in simmering water until they float to the top. With a slotted spoon, lift them out of the water *gently*. Transfer to a cold waterbath. Before serving, reheat in a pot of boiling water and remove again with a slotted spoon.

4. Make fried leeks: Rinse the leeks and pat them completely dry. Heat canola oil until very hot, add the leeks, and fry for 35 to 40 seconds, or until golden brown. Drain on paper towels and add salt.

5. To serve, place 5 *gnocchi* in each of 6 warm soup bowls, pour in the bouillon, and garnish with the chives, grated goat cheese, and fried leeks.

HINT FROM THE CHEF: It is best to use Yukon potatoes as they are yellow in color and are creamier in texture than Idaho potatoes.

SERVES 6

SALADS

La Caravelle, legendary for its classic French gastronomy, has responded to the more health-conscious American eater with this crabmeat salad, lightly infused with oils and drizzled with a spicy gazpacho sauce. The crunchy texture of the cucumbers and the zesty orange make a luscious combination with the tender crab morsels.

CRABMEAT AND CUCUMBER SALAD WITH DILL AND ROSEMARY OILS

LA CARAVELLE

GAZPACHO SAUCE

2 to 3 tomatoes, blanched, peeled, and seeded

3 fresh plum tomatoes, blanched, peeled, and seeded

2 stalks celery

2 red bell peppers, seeded

1 yellow bell pepper, seeded

3 shallots, peeled

1 garlic clove, peeled

1 teaspoon Tabasco

$^1/_2$ teaspoon Worcestershire sauce

$^1/_2$ teaspoon ketchup

sea salt and freshly ground white pepper to taste

CRABMEAT SALAD

1 pound fresh lump crabmeat, shell and cartilage removed

4 teaspoons orange zest

1 tablespoon chopped fresh fines herbes (chervil, chives, tarragon, parsley, and coriander leaves)

1 teaspoon Rosemary Oil (page 198)

4 tablespoons cucumber, peeled, seeded, and finely diced

1 teaspoon chopped fresh dill

1 teaspoon Dill Oil (page 198)

1 cup mesclun (mixed greens), washed, patted dry, and finely julienned

GARNISH

4 sprigs fresh dill

1. Make the gazpacho sauce: Place all the gazpacho ingredients in a juicer or blender and process until smooth. Pass through a fine strainer or *chinois* into a squeeze bottle and refrigerate until ready to use.

2. Combine the crabmeat, orange zest, chopped herbs, and season with salt and pepper to taste. Add the rosemary oil and combine.

3. In another bowl, mix the cucumber, chopped dill, dill oil, and a pinch of salt and pepper. Cover with plastic wrap. Do not marinate too long or the mixture will get soggy.

4. To serve, place a 3-inch metal ring on each large dinner plate and fill with *mesclun* one-third of the way up the sides. Add the crabmeat salad another one-third of the way up. Top with the finely diced cucumber mixture, leveling it with a knife. Remove the ring when ready to serve. Drizzle each plate with some of the gazpacho sauce and garnish with a sprig of dill.

SERVES 4

This earthy duck salad, filled with the intense flavors of confit and Roquefort, makes a tantalizing luncheon dish or an inspiring accompaniment to a fall or winter meal.

PRESERVED DUCK SALAD ROULADE WITH WARM ROQUEFORT VINAIGRETTE

AUREOLE

VINAIGRETTE
²/₃ cup extra-virgin olive oil
¹/₄ cup warm Dark Chicken Stock (page 203)
3 tablespoons peeled, minced shallots
¹/₃ cup red wine vinegar
salt and freshly ground black pepper to taste

SALAD
8 romaine leaves
2 medium tomatoes
1 small head frisée (*or white chicory*), washed and patted dry

3 legs Duck Confit, shredded (page 197)
2 shallots or baby onions, peeled and finely diced

GARNISH
1 tomato, seeded and diced
³/₄ cup crumbled Roquefort cheese
1 tablespoon chopped fresh parsley
4 tablespoons chive points (top 3 inches of the chives)

1. Make the vinaigrette: In a bowl, slowly whisk the oil into the warm chicken stock until emulsified. Gradually add the shallots, wine vinegar, and salt and pepper to taste.

2. Dip the romaine lettuce leaves in and out of boiling salted water to soften. Shock in cold water. Lay the romaine leaves on a sheet of parchment or wax paper and dry carefully with a clean cloth.

3. Blanch, peel, and seed the tomatoes and cut into strips.

4. In a bowl, toss the *frisée* (reserve some for garnishing the plates), shredded confit, shallots, and tomatoes with 2 tablespoons of the vinaigrette. Divide the mixture evenly among the romaine lettuce leaves, placing it in the center of each. Roll the leaves into tight, cigar-shaped rolls, about 2 inches wide, starting from the curled, leafy sides.

5. In a sauté pan, heat the remaining vinaigrette and gradually add the crumbled Roquefort, making sure the cheese does not boil. Keep warm.

6. To serve, place a small amount of *frisée* in the center of each plate. Cut the lettuce rolls into pieces on a slight diagonal and place on the plate. Sprinkle with diced tomato. Spoon the warm Roquefort dressing equally over the salads. Garnish each plate with parsley and chive points. Serve immediately with crunchy peasant bread or toasts.

N O T E :   Duck confit and other game delicacies can be purchased from D'Artagnan, located at 399 St. Paul Avenue, Jersey City, NJ 07306, or by calling 1(800) DARTAGN.

S E R V E S 4

This stunning salad, presented as an endive tent, has a surprise of warm goat cheese encased in crunchy phyllo dough. The tent is sprinkled with herbs and a confetti of diced red pepper.

ENDIVE SALAD WITH GOAT CHEESE AND CHIVES

LA GAULOISE

RATATOUILLE
1 red bell pepper, seeded
1 green bell pepper, seeded
1 zucchini
1 eggplant
salt and freshly ground pepper to taste

1 1/2 logs goat cheese (11 ounces per log)
1 tablespoon heavy cream
2 bunches chives, chopped
1/2 cup olive oil
*5 to 7 heads endive, rinsed, leaves
    separated, and patted dry*
6 sheets phyllo dough
1 bunch basil, stemmed and chopped

1 bunch rosemary, stemmed and chopped
1 bunch thyme, stemmed and chopped

VINAIGRETTE
1 cup extra-virgin olive oil
3 tablespoons red wine vinegar
2 tablespoons Dijon mustard
salt and freshly ground pepper to taste
*1/2 pound mesclun (mixed greens),
    washed, patted dry, and cut into
    1-inch pieces*

GARNISH
2 red bell peppers, finely diced

1. Make the ratatouille: Dice the peppers, zucchini, and eggplant into small cubes and sauté each vegetable separately in a pan with a small amount of olive oil until *al dente*. Mix the vegetables together in a large bowl and add salt and pepper to taste.

2. Cut six 1/2-inch pieces from the goat cheese logs and reserve. Make a paste by thoroughly mixing the remainder with the heavy cream, chopped chives, and olive oil. Spread a small amount of goat cheese paste on each endive leaf, reaching three-quarters of the way up the leaf.

3. Cut the sheets of phyllo dough in half to make 12 pieces. Brush with a small amount of olive oil and press 2 layers together. Place 2 tablespoons of the ratatouille in the center of each double sheet of phyllo dough. Place 1 slice of goat cheese on top of the ratatouille, then 1 tablespoon of olive oil, a few pieces of basil, some chopped rosemary, thyme, and salt and freshly ground pepper. Form a pouch by pressing together the corners of the phyllo sheets.

4. Preheat the oven to 500 degrees F. Coat a baking pan with 3 tablespoons olive oil and place the pouches on the pan. Bake until the phyllo starts to brown and crisp, at least 5 minutes. Discard the excess oil.

5. Make the vinaigrette: Slowly whisk the oil into the vinegar and mustard. Add salt and pepper to taste. Toss the *mesclun* with half of the vinaigrette.

6. To serve, place a 3-inch metal ring in the middle of each plate and pack with a handful of the salad. Remove the ring. Put the phyllo pouch on top of the salad and place the endive leaves around the salad like an Indian tent, so that the tips of the leaves touch each other on top. Press each endive leaf tightly one by one and build outward.

7. Add the remaining chopped herbs (approximately 2 tablespoons per portion) to the remaining vinaigrette and pour over the tents. Garnish with the diced red pepper.

SERVES 6

Fine strips of orange rind and orange vinaigrette accent this exquisitely arranged salad of tender, succulent lobster medallions. Haricots verts and colorful pepper diamonds create an unusual and elegant impression.

LOBSTER SALAD WITH BASIL-ORANGE DRESSING AND HARICOTS VERTS

LA GAULOISE

1 gallon Vegetable Stock (page 208)
six 1-pound female lobsters
2 navel oranges

VINAIGRETTE DRESSING
2 tablespoons Dijon mustard
3 tablespoons red wine vinegar
1 cup extra-virgin olive oil
salt and freshly ground white pepper to taste
2 cups freshly squeezed orange juice

2 bunches basil, stemmed and finely julienned

2 pounds French haricots verts

GARNISH
6 basil leaves
1 red bell pepper, seeded and cut into diamond shapes
1 green bell pepper, seeded and cut into diamond shapes
1 yellow bell pepper, seeded and cut into diamond shapes

1. In a large soup pot, bring the vegetable stock to a rapid boil. Add the lobsters—in batches if necessary—and cook for 5 minutes. Let cool and shell the lobsters, reserving the heads and roe. Thinly slice the lobster meat into medallions, maintaining the shape of the tail piece.

2. Remove the skin from the oranges and separate them into segments. Blanch in boiling water for 5 minutes. Drain and julienne. Reserve.

3. Make the vinaigrette: In a bowl, mix together the mustard and vinegar and whisk in the oil. Season with salt and white pepper.

4. In a saucepan, reduce the orange juice until syrupy and place in a bowl. Gradually whisk in half the vinaigrette. Add the orange segments and the basil julienne and combine. Season with salt and pepper to taste.

5. Blanch the *haricots verts* in boiling salted water until *al dente*. Shock in cold water. Toss in a bowl with the remaining vinaigrette and season with salt and pepper to taste.

6. To serve, place a 3-inch round metal ring on each dinner plate. Pack with a layer of *haricots verts* and top with a layer of lobster meat, overlapping the pieces. Remove the ring and spoon the vinaigrette around each plate. Sprinkle the orange rind julienne on top. Garnish each plate with lobster roe, a whole basil leaf, and orange segments. Place 1 lobster head on the side of each plate and decorate each plate rim with the pepper diamonds.

SERVES 6

This pomegranate-glazed quail salad exhibits a complex rendering of flavors and textures, and although somewhat time-consuming to prepare is well worth the effort. The berries of the thick-skinned plum pomegranate, the old Roman name for the "apple of Carthage," combine here with citrus juice to produce a sumptuous glaze. Chef Bobby Flay presents this Southwestern quail delicacy with great panache.

POMEGRANATE-GLAZED QUAIL SALAD WITH WALNUT OIL DRESSING

MESA GRILL

1 CUP POMEGRANATE GLAZE
1 1/2 cups pomegranate juice or 3/4 cup pomegranate concentrate
1/2 cup cranberry juice
1/2 cup freshly squeezed lime juice
1/2 cup freshly squeezed orange juice
2 tablespoons honey

WALNUT OIL DRESSING
2 tablespoons chopped red onion
1/2 cup red wine vinegar
2 teaspoons Dijon mustard
3/4 cup olive oil
3/4 cup walnut oil
salt and freshly ground white pepper to taste

6 quail, cut in half, breastbones and backbones removed
1 pound mesclun (mixed greens), washed and patted dry
salt and freshly ground black pepper to taste

GARNISH
1 cup ripe pomegranate seeds
1 cup walnuts, halved, optional
2 cups croutons, cut in 1-inch cubes
1 bunch chives, finely chopped
1 red bell pepper, seeded and finely diced
1/2 bunch cilantro

1. Make the pomegranate glaze: In a saucepan, combine all the glaze ingredients if using pomegranate juice and reduce by two-thirds until the liquid forms a syrup. If using pomegranate concentrate, add it to the saucepan after reducing the ingredients by two-thirds and then reduce again until a thick syrup forms. Cool. Pour the syrup into a blender to emulsify. Reserve.

2. Make the walnut oil dressing: In a blender, combine the onion, vinegar, and mustard, and blend until smooth. Slowly add the olive oil to emulsify. Add the walnut oil and process briefly. Add salt and pepper to taste.

3. Brush both the grill and the quail with oil to prevent sticking. Season the quail with salt and pepper. Grill the quail, skin-side down, over hot coals on a grill or on a preheated stovetop grill until tender, approximately 4 to 5 minutes. Turn the quail over, brush with the glaze, and cook an additional 2 to 3 minutes.

4. In a mixing bowl, dress the *mesclun* lightly with the walnut oil dressing and toss.

5. To serve, divide *mesclun* mixture among 6 dinner plates. Place 1 glazed quail on top so that the feet touch one another, standing up. Artfully sprinkle pomegranate seeds, walnuts, and croutons around the plate. Garnish with chopped chives, red pepper dice, and 3 or 4 cilantro leaves.

SERVES 6

This warm rabbit and sweetbread salad, with a satiny balsamic vinaigrette, originated in southern France, where the cuisine is pleasing and representative of the intoxicating beauty of Provence itself.

RABBIT AND SWEETBREADS IN AUTUMN GREENS

PARK BISTRO

¹/₂ pound sweetbreads

4 rabbit legs

salt and freshly ground white pepper to taste

6 tablespoons olive oil

1 head garlic, halved, with skin

1 bay leaf

2 onions, peeled and diced

1 branch fresh thyme

1 cup dry white wine

¹/₂ cup soy sauce

¹/₂ cup water

1 celeriac root, peeled and finely minced

1 bunch Italian parsley, stemmed and chopped

4 tablespoons balsamic vinegar

VINAIGRETTE

2 tablespoons balsamic vinegar

1 teaspoon white pepper

salt to taste

6 tablespoons extra-virgin olive oil

2 tablespoons finely chopped chives

2 heads endive

1 cup mâche *(tender spoon-shaped leaves of lamb's lettuce)*

GARNISH

4 branches tarragon

1. Preheat the oven to 450 degrees F.

2. In a pot of cold water, cook the sweetbreads until they come to a boil. Drain and run under cold water. When cool, remove the membranes and pull apart into bite-size pieces.

3. Season the rabbit legs with salt and white pepper. In a large, heavy, ovenproof skillet, heat 3 tablespoons of olive oil until very hot and sauté the rabbit legs over a high heat until golden brown. Reduce the heat to low, add the garlic, bay leaf, onions, and thyme, and cook until the onion turns golden brown. Place the skillet in the oven and roast the rabbit for 15 minutes. Return the skillet to the stove and deglaze with the wine, soy sauce, and water. Return the skillet to the oven and braise for 10 additional minutes. Remove the rabbit and pull the meat off the bones into small bite-size pieces. Strain the braising liquid into a bowl.

4. In a small bowl, combine the minced celeriac and parsley. Add to the braising liquid.

5. In a saucepan, sauté the sweetbreads and rabbit in 1 tablespoon of very hot olive oil until golden brown. Remove the meat. Off the heat, deglaze the pan with the balsamic vinegar. Return to the stove, and reduce by half over low heat. Add the braising liquid, and reduce by half. Add 2 tablespoons olive oil and return the meats to the sauce to warm.

6. Make the vinaigrette: In a salad bowl, combine the balsamic vinegar with white pepper and salt to taste. Whisk in the olive oil and then the chives.

7. Trim the bottom of each endive leaf and then cut in half lengthwise. Toss the *mâche* with the vinaigrette right before serving.

8. To serve, place the endive leaves on the outer circle of a dinner plate with the tips facing outward three-quarters of the way around the plate, like a crown. Place *mâche* in the center of each plate and arrange the rabbit and sweetbreads in the middle. Spoon the sauce over the meats and endive. Garnish by arranging a tarragon branch vertically in the rabbit and sweetbreads.

SERVES 4

VEGETABLES

According to folklore, artichokes à la Polita originated with Theodora, wife of Justinian I, Emperor of the Byzantine Empire. Since the majority of Greeks observe Lent, vegetarian main courses are popular, and these easy-to-prepare artichokes make a satisfying vegetarian entrée or a fine accompaniment to lamb or other roasted meats.

The neoclassical decor of Karyatis would suit the likes of Aristotle and Heroditus. It features a magnificent frieze portraying the Caryatides, from the Sacred Erechtheum on the Acropolis in Athens.

ARTICHOKES A LA POLITA

KARYATIS

6 artichokes

10 cups water

2 tablespoons flour

juice and rind of 1 lemon

6 red potatoes, peeled and halved

4 carrots, peeled and diced diagonally
 into $1/4$-inch slices

3 large onions, peeled and quartered

$1/3$ bunch dill, stemmed and chopped
 into 2-inch pieces

3 cups olive oil

3 cups fresh lemon juice

$1/2$ teaspoon salt

$1/3$ teaspoon white pepper

GARNISH
1 lemon, sliced

1. Preheat the oven to 250 degrees F.

2. Remove the outer leaves of each artichoke and scoop out the choke with a teaspoon. Trim all but 2 inches of the stem. To prevent the artichokes from discoloring, drop them into 4 cups of water mixed with the flour, and the juice and rind of the lemon, until ready to use.

3. Combine all the remaining vegetables and the dill in a roasting pan. Add the artichokes. In a small bowl, combine the olive oil, 6 cups water, 3 cups lemon juice, salt and pepper. Pour the liquid over the vegetables. Cover with aluminum foil and bake for 1 hour.

4. To serve, arrange the vegetables in 6 large-rimmed soup plates and divide the braising liquid among them. Garnish each serving with a slice or two of lemon.

SERVES 6

CRISP POTATO AND EGGPLANT TART

AUREOLE

1¹/₂ cups peeled and finely diced eggplant

3 tablespoons kosher salt

freshly ground white pepper to taste

4 tablespoons vegetable oil or Clarified
    Butter (page 196)

2 tablespoons minced shallots

3 large Idaho potatoes, peeled

4 tablespoons sweet butter

1. In a bowl, season the diced eggplant with 2 tablespoons salt and pepper and let rest for 20 minutes to draw out the water. Place in a towel and squeeze out the excess water.

2. Heat a medium saucepan until hot and add 2 tablespoons vegetable oil or clarified butter. Sauté the eggplant and minced shallots until tender. Set aside.

3. Shred the potatoes on a towel and squeeze out as much of the water as possible. Then season with the remaining kosher salt and freshly ground white pepper.

4. Heat an 8-inch sauté pan and add the remaining 2 tablespoons vegetable oil or clarified butter. Place half the potatoes in the pan, pressing down on them with a spatula, and spread the eggplant evenly over them. Place the remaining potatoes on top, pressing firmly and leaving a ¹/₄-inch border from the edge of the pan. Cover and cook the tart until golden brown on the bottom. Dab the top with butter, turn the tart over, and cook until browned, about 12 minutes. Finish cooking in a preheated 375 degree F. oven for up to 15 minutes.

5. To serve, cut the tart into quarters with a serrated knife and serve hot and crispy.

HINTS FROM THE CHEF: It is important to wrap the diced eggplant in a towel to squeeze out its bitter liquid. Moreover, Idaho potatoes have a high starch content and as soon as they are shredded, they must be squeezed out in a towel to prevent oxidation; sauté them immediately.

SERVES 4

This crisp potato and eggplant tart is one of the most sought-after vegetable dishes in town. It reflects Charles Palmer's lighter approach to classic flavors and is a variation on the French potato tart pommes Anna *or* galette de pommes de terre.

Chef Palmer is known not only for his inventive cuisine, but also for his masterful presentations. He rarely uses cream in his food, with the exception of a few desserts.

The Palm's hash browns have been one of its signature dishes for many decades. Served with a succulent charcoal grilled steak or an oversized lobster, these potatoes are a delight.

The Palm Restaurant opened its doors as a speakeasy in 1926, when the Bozzi and Ganzi families came to this country from Parma, Italy. It has been said that the immigration clerk wrote down Palm instead of Parma, and thus the restaurant began its successful journey. The Palm enjoys nationwide popularity with restaurants in Washington, D.C., Easthampton, Long Island, Houston, Dallas, and Los Angeles.

I have a particular fondness for The Palm in New York since a caricature of my grandfather, the late Joseph Gantz, once a prominent Port Chester, New York brush manufacturer, hangs on the wall along with such celebrated personalities as Yogi Berra, J. Edgar Hoover, Francis Ford Coppola, and Jackie Gleason.

HASH BROWN POTATOES

THE PALM RESTAURANT

8 large new red potatoes
1 cup Clarified Butter (page 196)
1 teaspoon salt
freshly ground black pepper to taste

1. Cook the potatoes in 2 quarts of salted boiling water for 7 minutes. Dry the potatoes and let them cool.

2. Place the potatoes over a wide metal mesh strainer or sieve and press down on them with the palms of your hands. (Some of the skins will come off on the mesh and can be discarded.)

3. In a warm 7-inch nonstick or steel-carbon saucepan, heat the clarified butter until very hot. Place the potatoes in the pan and season with the salt and freshly ground pepper to taste. Brown nicely on both sides, cooking for approximately 10 minutes. Serve hot.

SERVES 4

ENDIVE WITH GORGONZOLA

DA UMBERTO

4 tablespoons extra-virgin olive oil

6 to 8 endives, cut in half lengthwise

2 tablespoons white wine vinegar

salt and freshly ground black pepper to
taste

1/4 pound gorgonzola, cut into chunks

1. Preheat the oven to 450 degrees F.

2. Into a roasting pan, pour 2 tablespoons of the olive oil. Arrange the endives in the pan with the inner leaves facing up. Sprinkle with the remaining 2 tablespoons olive oil, the vinegar, and salt and pepper to taste.

3. Cook the endives for 15 minutes. Sprinkle the gorgonzola over the endives and return the pan to the oven for 2 to 3 minutes, or until the cheese melts. Serve warm or cold.

HINT FROM THE CHEF: *Parmigiano Reggiano* can be substituted for the gorgonzola or combined with the gorgonzola for the topping.

SERVES 4

This northern Italian dish makes a luscious vegetable serving or an antipasto. The gorgonzola, a ripe Italian blue cheese, brings out the pungent, anise-like flavor of the endive. Da Umberto, a classic Florentine trattoria, *serves the endive along with* caponata, *caramelized onions, and grilled eggplant.*

*Sweet onion and anchovy tart,
topped with niçoise olives, and
otherwise known in France as
pissaladière, is a specialty of Nice,
where the sun warms the pebbled
beaches and an azure sea
illuminates the sky.*

PROVENCALE SWEET ONION AND ANCHOVY TART

PROVENCE

¹/₂ ounce dry cake or baker's yeast or ¹/₂
    tablespoon granular yeast
1 teaspoon sugar
¹/₂ cup lukewarm water
1¹/₈ cups all-purpose flour
2 teaspoons kosher salt
¹/₄ cup olive oil
3 medium red onions, peeled

1 teaspoon minced garlic
2 teaspoons herbes de Provence
salt and freshly ground black pepper to
    taste
4 very large red tomatoes
24 pitted black niçoise olives
24 anchovy filets

1. In a large bowl, mix together the yeast, sugar, and warm water, stir well, and let "proof" for 20 minutes in a warm place.

2. In the bowl of an electric mixer, add the flour, salt, and ¹/₂ tablespoon oil to the yeast mixture and knead with the dough hook until the dough develops a smooth texture and springs back when touched, approximately 8 to 10 minutes. Let rest for 3 minutes. Transfer the dough to a large bowl and keep warm by covering with a wet towel until it doubles in volume, about 2 hours. Remove the dough from the bowl to a floured surface, punch it down, and let rest. Transfer the dough to a large bowl, cover the bowl with a damp towel, and allow dough to rise in a warm place until it doubles in volume, about 2 hours.

3. Preheat the oven to 350 degrees F.

4. With half of the remaining oil, moisten a 6- × 9-inch baking pan. Flatten the dough to fit the dimensions of the baking pan; press the dough pieces into the pan evenly. Bake the dough for 18 to 20 minutes.

5. Coat another baking pan with the remaining olive oil. Slice the red onions into thin ¹/₈-inch slices and arrange them overlapping in both horizontal and vertical rows in the pan. Sprinkle them with the minced garlic, the *herbes de Provence*, and salt and pepper to taste. Then slice the tomatoes, and place them on top of the onions so that they also overlap. Bake the onions and tomatoes (at 350 degrees F.) until tender, about 25 minutes. While still warm, invert the pan with the dough upside down onto the onion/tomato pan, pressing both pans together. Turn the pans over so that the onions and tomatoes are on top. Remove the top pan and top the tart with the olives and anchovies. Reheat the tart just before you are ready to serve so that it is piping hot.

SERVES 6

Shun Lee has been continually acclaimed as one of the best Chinese restaurants in New York City. While known for bringing Hunan cooking to New York, proprietor Michael Tong excels in specialties from all regions in China.

Instead of meat or pork, these dry sautéed string beans contain minced pickles, which add spark to one of my favorite vegetable dishes.

DRY SAUTEED STRING BEANS

SHUN LEE

2 teaspoons soy sauce

2 teaspoons sugar

4 cups vegetable or soy bean oil

1¹/₂ pounds string beans, trimmed

6 tablespoons Light Chicken Stock
  (page 203)

2 tablespoons sherry

6 scallions, with stems and bulbs, finely
  chopped

4 tablespoons finely chopped Szechuan
  pickles

1 tablespoon sesame oil

1. Mix soy sauce and sugar together in a small bowl.

2. Heat all but 1 tablespoon of the vegetable or soy bean oil in a large wok. When very hot (approximately 300 degrees F.), add the string beans and cook for about 3 minutes. Stir with a large metal spoon until the oil becomes opaque.

3. With a strainer, carefully remove the beans from the hot oil and immediately top the beans with the remaining tablespoon of oil. (Keep the beans in the strainer until you are ready to return them to the wok.) There should be very little oil remaining in the wok; pour off what remains and reserve for future Chinese cooking.

4. In the wok, heat the chicken broth, sherry, and soy-sugar mixture and add the scallions, Szechuan pickles, and then the string beans. Stir-fry with the sesame oil, cooking no more than 5 minutes.

HINTS FROM THE CHEF: The key to Chinese cooking is to use a very high flame and cook quickly. The food must be crisp and tender. Make sure not to overcook anything.

SERVES 4

MASHED TURNIPS WITH CRISPY SHALLOTS

UNION SQUARE CAFE

6 cups soy or peanut oil

2 sticks sweet butter

12 large shallots, peeled and sliced into
    thin rounds

3 pounds rutabagas (yellow turnips)

1 tablespoon salt

1 cup heavy cream

kosher salt and freshly ground black
    pepper to taste

GARNISH

1 bunch parsley, stemmed and chopped

These luscious creamy yellow turnips (otherwise known as rutabagas), studded with crispy shallots, have been called "drop dead great" and the "Madonna of restaurant vegetables" by New York Newsday. Many people frequent the Union Square Cafe for its highly sought-after vegetable combinations.

1. Make the crispy shallots: Cook the oil and 1 stick of butter in a large saucepan over high heat until the mixture begins to bubble. Reduce the heat and add the shallots; cook slowly for approximately 30 to 45 minutes, stirring occasionally, until golden brown. Strain the shallots into a fine colander, flatten them on an absorbent towel, and keep in a warm place for about 3 hours. (The shallots can be prepared a day in advance.)

2. Peel the rutabagas, cut them in half lengthwise, then cut both halves into 4 pieces. (Altogether each rutabaga should be cut into eighths.) Place in a large soup pot, add salted water to cover, and boil for approximately 35 to 40 minutes, until soft. Drain and then purée in a food processor until smooth and creamy, approximately 3 minutes.

3. Melt the remaining stick of butter in a saucepan. In a separate saucepan, heat the cream until it is warm.

4. In a large saucepan over low heat, heat the rutabaga purée and gradually incorporate the butter and cream to taste, stirring constantly with a wooden spoon.

5. Season the rutabaga purée with salt and pepper to taste and serve topped with the crispy shallots and garnished with chopped parsley.

SERVES 6

Chef Michael Romano's Italian heritage and firm grounding in French culinary traditions are illustrated here in this tasty, crustless "little torte." Romano was recently named one of America's top ten new chefs by Food & Wine *magazine and Union Square Cafe garnered a DiRōNA Award, the acronym for Distinguished Restaurants of North America.*

Vegetable tortino is popular throughout northern Italy and can be served as an appetizer, main course, or side dish. As a main course, it is enticing served in a light pool of tomato sauce; as a side dish, it makes a satisfying accompaniment to a succulent grilled veal chop.

VEGETABLE TORTINO WITH PARMESAN CRUST

UNION SQUARE CAFE

10 tablespoons olive oil

1 pound Spanish onions, peeled and cut into $^1/_8$-inch slices

salt and freshly ground white pepper to taste

1 pound eggplant, peeled, quartered lengthwise, and cut into $^1/_4$-inch cubes

$^1/_2$ pound zucchini, washed and sliced into $^1/_8$-inch rounds

$^1/_2$ pound yellow squash, washed and sliced into $^1/_8$-inch rounds

BATTER

5 eggs

4 tablespoons olive oil

2 tablespoons balsamic vinegar

1 cup cream

6 ounces Parmigiano Reggiano, grated

TOPPING

2 ounces Parmigiano Reggiano, grated

1. Make the onion confit: Preheat the oven to 400 degrees F. In a medium sauté pan, heat 4 tablespoons of the olive oil; add onions and cook gently over low heat until very tender, but not browned. Season with salt and pepper to taste. Cook in the oven until caramelized, approximately $1^1/_4$ hours.

2. Lightly oil a large cookie sheet. Arrange eggplant cubes fitted closely together on sheet and brush with oil. Reduce the oven temperature to 350 degrees F. and roast for 1 hour.

3. In a large sauté pan, heat 4 tablespoons of the olive oil and sauté the zucchini and yellow squash slices over high heat until tender. Season with salt and pepper to taste. Using a colander, drain off the excess liquid.

4. Make the batter: In a large mixing bowl—by hand or by food processor—process the batter ingredients to form a thick, homogenous liquid.

5. Oil a 2-inch-deep, 2-quart baking dish with the remaining 2 tablespoons olive oil and alternate layers of onions, eggplant, zucchini, and yellow squash. Mix in the liquid and stir with a spoon to incorporate. Cover with fork-punctured foil and bake at 300 degrees F. for 1 hour. Remove the foil and bake for an additional 15 minutes. Top with *Parmigiano Reggiano* and brown the top by placing briefly under a hot broiler.

SERVES 4 TO 6

SQUASH PUREE

LA COTE BASQUE

2 to 3 medium butternut squash

2 medium sweet potatoes, peeled

1 small onion, peeled and cut into small
dices

3 tablespoons sweet butter

$^1/_2$ cup Crème Fraîche (page 196)

pinch of nutmeg

salt and freshly ground white pepper to
taste

1. Preheat the oven to 225 degrees F.

2. Carefully peel off the tough skin of the squash with a paring knife. Cut the squash in half lengthwise and scoop out the seeds and pulp.

3. In a pot of rapidly boiling water, cook the squash and potatoes until tender, approximately 20 to 25 minutes. Drain the vegetables, place them in a roasting pan, and heat them in the oven for approximately 10 minutes, or until they dry out.

4. Meanwhile, melt the butter in a skillet and sweat the onions over low heat until translucent. Cut the squash and potatoes into large chunks. In a food processor, purée the squash and potatoes with the onion and add the remaining ingredients. Process well and adjust the seasoning.

5. To serve, spoon the purée into a pastry bag fitted with a #6 tip and pipe onto dinner plates in oval shapes or other attractive designs.

SERVES 5

Vegetable purées have long been one of La Côte Basque's trademarks and a mainstay of classic French cuisine. Chef-proprietor Jean-Jacques Rachou has excelled at preparing purées for over forty years.

The squash purée provides a sensational accompaniment for game or any full-flavored dish, particularly in the autumn. The pear and spinach purée makes a singularly good combination, as well, and uses rice instead of cream as a binder. Other interesting combinations to try include cauliflower and potato, and sweet potato and carrot.

Inviting murals of the French fishing village of Saint-Jean-de-Luz set the scene for the prodigious culinary delights served at La Côte Basque.

PEAR AND SPINACH PUREE

LA COTE BASQUE

6 Bosc pears, peeled

1 cup dry white wine

pinch of nutmeg

1 cup basmati rice

1 pound fresh spinach, well rinsed to
  remove all sand and grit

cinnamon to taste

2 tablespoons sweet butter

salt and freshly ground white pepper to
  taste

1. In a medium saucepan over high heat, bring 1 cup water and the wine to a boil. Add the pears with the nutmeg and poach for approximately 20 minutes, or until tender. Let the pears marinate in the syrup overnight. Remove the pears, pat them completely dry, and discard the syrup.

2. Cook the rice: Rinse the rice in several changes of water, then soak for 20 minutes. In a saucepan bring the rice and $1^1/2$ cups water to a boil, reduce the heat to low, and cook, covered, until tender, approximately 25 minutes.

3. Cook the spinach in a pot of rapidly boiling water for 3 minutes. Drain well and with your hands squeeze out all the water. Dry with paper towels.

4. Core and stem the pears, place them and the spinach in a food processor, and process well for approximately 5 minutes. Add the rice, season with cinnamon or nutmeg, and process until smooth. Transfer the purée to a bowl and whisk in the butter. Season with salt and pepper to taste.

5. To serve, spoon the mixture into a pastry bag fitted with a #6 tip and pipe artfully onto each plate.

HINTS FROM THE CHEF: The pear and spinach purée is a little more difficult to make than other purées because the spinach turns brown if cooked too long, and you must pat the pears and spinach dry, because they have a high water content. If you are serving this purée with game, it is preferable to use cinnamon instead of nutmeg. Basmati rice works better than regular American rice because it is thinner, whiter, and more flavorful.

SERVES 6

PASTAS AND GRAINS

This flavorful linguine, bathed in aromatic natural clam juices, bursts with the enticing aroma of garlic. Garlic has been a popular seasoning for over 4,000 years and is believed to be beneficial for blood circulation and the heart. Legend has it that garlic, the "spear of god," kept away evil spirits.

LINGUINE WITH CLAM SAUCE

IL MONELLO

32 littleneck clams
3 tablespoons olive oil
6 garlic cloves, peeled and crushed
pinch of fresh oregano
pinch of crushed dried hot red pepper
  flakes

3 cups fresh clam juice or Fish Stock
  (page 204)
2 pounds linguine
2 tablespoons chopped fresh Italian
  parsley
1 tablespoon chopped fresh basil leaves

1. Wash the clams well by scrubbing them in cold water, then rubbing them together to remove any sand. Make sure all are closed, which indicates that they are alive.

2. Remove 12 clams from their shells and mince them, reserving the juices.

3. Heat the olive oil in a large saucepan and sauté the garlic. Add the clams, the minced clams, the reserved clam juice, the oregano, the crushed red pepper, and the clam juice or fish stock. As soon as the clams open, remove them to another pan and keep warm, covered. Cook the sauce over medium heat for 5 minutes.

4. Meanwhile, cook the linguine in rapidly boiling salted water until *al dente* and drain. Add the linguine to the sauce along with the chopped parsley and basil. Toss for a few minutes until heated through and the linguine absorbs all the flavors in the pan.

5. Garnish each serving of linguine with clams in the shell and their juice. Serve hot.

HINT FROM THE CHEF: Fish stock is preferable to bottled clam juice because the stock is less salty and more flavorful. As the clams open up, they will also add juice to the sauce.

SERVES 4 AS A FIRST COURSE

PAHT THAI

Rice Noodles Stir-Fried Thai Style

T O M M Y   T A N G ' S

³/₄ pound dried rice noodles

8 cups cold water

¹/₂ C U P   T A M A R I N D   J U I C E

  ¹/₄ cup tamarind pulp

  ¹/₂ cup warm water

¹/₄ cup vegetable oil

1 tablespoon chopped garlic

16 medium shrimp, shelled and deveined

*¹/₄ cup firm brown tofu, cut into ¹/₄-inch
  dice*

2 eggs

¹/₄ cup dry roasted peanuts, crushed

3 tablespoons Thai fish sauce

2¹/₂ tablespoons white rice vinegar

*1 tablespoon sugar or 1¹/₂ tablespoons
  honey*

2 teaspoons sweet Hungarian paprika

*¹/₂ teaspoon crushed dried red pepper
  flakes or cayenne pepper*

3 ounces fresh bean sprouts

G A R N I S H

*¹/₄ cup leeks, cut into 1¹/₂- to 2-inch
  shreds*

1 lime, cut into wedges

*While Thai cooking is known for
its ginger carvings and vegetable
flower garnishes, that type of formal
presentation is reserved for the
nobility. This flavorful home-
cooked style of Paht Thai
demonstrates the Thai affection for
chilies, tamarind, tofu, and fish
sauce. The citrus from the lime and
the crunchy bean sprouts provide a
soothing contrast to the rice noodles,
which are bountiful in central
Thailand.*

1. Soak the rice noodles in cold water for 45 minutes. Drain and set aside.

2. Make the tamarind juice: In a small bowl, soak the tamarind pulp in the warm water for approximately 30 minutes then mash to form a paste. Press the pulp through a strainer with a bowl underneath to catch the juice. Reserve the juice.

3. In a large wok or skillet, heat the oil until almost smoking and sauté the garlic until slightly browned, approximately 1 minute.

4. Add the shrimp and tofu and sauté for 1 minute. Stir in the raw eggs and cook for 30 seconds. Add the reserved noodles, tamarind juice, peanuts, fish sauce, vinegar, sugar, paprika, and red pepper and stir-fry constantly for 3 minutes.

5. To serve, sprinkle with the bean sprouts and garnish with shredded leeks and lime wedges.

N O T E :   Tamarind imported from Thailand is highly recommended. If unavailable, substitute ¹/₄ cup lemon juice.

S E R V E S   4

WHOLE WHEAT PAPPARDELLE
WITH PORCINI SAUCE

FELIDIA

1 pound fresh Whole Wheat Pappardelle
 (page 199)

1/4 cup olive oil

1 pound fresh porcini mushrooms, or a
 mixture with morels or shiitake,
 trimmed and sliced

4 garlic cloves, peeled and lightly crushed

salt and freshly ground black pepper to
 taste

2 tablespoons sweet butter, optional

3 tablespoons chopped Italian parsley

3/4 cup Light Chicken Stock (page 203)

3 tablespoons dry white wine

1/2 cup grated Parmigiano Reggiano

These delicate, broad ribbon noodles made with whole wheat flour strike the perfect balance with this earthy, flavorful porcini mushroom sauce. Chef-proprietor Lidia Bastianich is not only a star in her own kitchen, but also lectures eloquently and passionately about Italian food and its derivation.

1. Bring 6 quarts of water with 1 tablespoon salt to a boil.

2. Make the *porcini* sauce: In a large skillet, heat the olive oil, and sauté the garlic until browned. Add the *porcini* mushrooms and garlic cloves and season with salt and pepper to taste. Sauté until the mushrooms are lightly browned on both sides, turning gently with a spatula. Transfer the *porcini* to a plate and keep warm.

3. Discard the excess oil from the pan and add butter, if desired, and parsley. Adjust the seasoning. Add the chicken stock and wine and simmer over medium heat for approximately 10 minutes.

4. Cook the pappardelle in boiling water for 2 minutes, at the most, stirring with a wooden spoon. Meanwhile, add the reserved *porcini* to the sauce. Drain the pasta well and add it to the sauce, tossing gently. Stir in the *Parmigiano*. Serve immediately.

HINT FROM THE CHEF: Fresh pappardelle cook so quickly that they should be added to rapidly boiling water just before the sauce is finished.

SERVES 4

Touted as the best restaurant in America by Forbes *magazine and* The New York Times, *Le Cirque remains one of the most magical of New York restaurants, and Sirio Maccioni is one of the world's greatest hosts. It has been said that Le Cirque invented* pasta primavera. *A bounty of fresh vegetables adorns the pasta, in a sensuously delicious cream sauce.*

PASTA PRIMAVERA

LE CIRQUE

7 tablespoons extra-virgin olive oil

pinch of salt

1 gallon water or Light Chicken Stock (see page 203)

1/2 cup shelled fresh peas

1 cup broccoli florets

1 medium zucchini, halved and sliced 1/4 inch thick

1/2 cup green beans, preferably haricots verts, trimmed and cut into 1-inch pieces

12 thin asparagus, cut into 1-inch pieces

2 tablespoons pine nuts

1 cup mushrooms, thinly sliced

1 teaspoon finely chopped jalapeño pepper or 1/2 teaspoon crushed dried red pepper flakes

salt and freshly ground pepper to taste

1 tablespoon finely minced garlic

4 fresh ripe plum tomatoes, seeded and cut into 1/2-inch cubes

3 sprigs basil leaves only, finely chopped

3 tablespoons sweet butter

2 tablespoons Light Chicken Stock (page 203)

3/4 cup heavy cream

3 tablespoons mascarpone cheese

1/4 cup grated Parmesan cheese (1 ounce)

1 pound pasta, preferably spaghetti

2 tablespoons chopped chives

GARNISH

whole basil leaves

1. Add 1 tablespoon of the olive oil and a pinch of salt to 1 gallon of water or light chicken stock and bring to a rapid boil. Let simmer until ready to cook the pasta.

2. In a 1 1/2- to 2-quart saucepan, bring a quart of water with 1/2 tablespoon of salt to a rapid boil. Add the fresh peas and cook for 1 minute. Drain the peas and run under very cold water. Set aside.

3. Repeat the same procedure as above, cooking the broccoli, zucchini, green beans, and asparagus separately, each for approximately 5 minutes, or until *al dente*.

4. In a large sauté pan, heat 2 tablespoons of the olive oil over high heat and toast the pine nuts until light brown. Remove and reserve. To the same pan, add the mushrooms, broccoli, zucchini, green beans, asparagus, and jalapeño pepper, and cook, stirring, for 6 minutes. Season with salt and pepper to taste. Stir in the peas and set aside.

5. Heat 1 tablespoon of the remaining olive oil in a small saucepan over medium heat and sauté half the minced garlic for 2 minutes. Then add the tomatoes and salt and freshly ground black pepper to taste, and cook another 3 to 4 minutes. Add the basil and set aside.

6. In a large saucepan, heat 3 tablespoons olive oil and sauté the remaining garlic. Add the vegetable mixture and cook until heated through.

7. In a medium saucepan, melt the butter and add the chicken stock, heavy cream, *mascarpone* and Parmesan cheeses, a pinch of salt, and freshly ground black pepper, and cook over low heat for 5 minutes.

8. Cook the pasta in rapidly boiling water (Step 1). Stir and cook for 5 to 7 minutes, or until *al dente*. Drain.

9. Place the pasta in a large skillet, add the cream sauce, and blend over medium heat. Add half of the vegetable mixture and all of the tomato mixture. Toss well for 2 minutes, making sure the mixture is piping hot. Add the chives and reserved pine nuts and toss.

10. To serve, place pasta with sauce on each plate, and pour remaining vegetables over the pasta. Garnish each serving with a whole basil leaf.

N O T E :   If using spaghetti, fresh pasta is recommended. However, if using penne or other tubular pastas, Italian dried pasta is preferred. It is very important to serve the pasta piping hot. Always add the cooked pasta to the saucepan with the hot vegetable sauce at the last minute. Parmesan cheese should be freshly grated and preferably imported from Parma, Italy. Grated Parmesan can be kept in a plastic bag or air-tight container in the freezer for up to 6 months. Extra-virgin olive oil is essential to this dish because it is richer and more flavorful than lesser-grade olive oils. Garlic should never color when cooked; otherwise it will have a bitter flavor.

S E R V E S   4

*When twenty-seven-year-old
Debra Ponzek became Montrachet's
chef, she received rave reviews and
was named one of America's ten
best new chefs by* Food & Wine
magazine, and chef of the year by
Chefs of America.

*It has been said that Marcella
Hazan, the high priestess of
northern Italian cooking, praises
Montrachet's pasta with wild
mushrooms as the best pasta dish
in New York City. Every morsel of
these miniature pasta bow ties,
tossed with earthy mushrooms and
scented with a creamy truffle juice
sauce, should be savored.*

BOW TIE PASTA WITH WILD MUSHROOMS AND TRUFFLE JUICE

MONTRACHET

2 tablespoons olive oil

2 stalks celery, finely diced

1 carrot, peeled and finely diced

8 shallots, peeled and finely diced

1 cup wild mushroom stems or domestic
    mushrooms, finely diced

1 cup Light Chicken Stock (page 203)

$1^1/2$ cups heavy cream

salt and freshly ground white pepper to
    taste

$2^1/2$ cups uncooked tripolini (small bow
    tie pasta)

$^3/4$ pound shiitake mushrooms, thinly
    sliced

6 tablespoons juice of black truffles or
    truffle oil

kosher salt to taste

GARNISH
6 tablespoons finely chopped chives

1. Make the cream sauce: In a large saucepan, heat the olive oil until hot and lightly sauté the celery, carrot, and shallots for 3 to 4 minutes. Add the finely diced mushroom stems or domestic mushrooms and stir. Add the chicken stock and simmer for 10 minutes. Add the heavy cream and simmer over medium heat, stirring occasionally, for 20 minutes, or until slightly thickened. The cream should lightly coat the back of a spoon.

2. Strain the sauce through a fine sieve into a bowl, season with salt and pepper to taste, and return to the pan.

3. Cook the pasta in rapidly boiling salted water for 3 to 5 minutes, until *al dente*, and drain.

4. Meanwhile, add the sliced mushrooms and truffle juice to the cream sauce and cook over medium heat until the mushrooms are slightly wilted. There should be very little liquid remaining.

5. Add the cooked pasta to the cream sauce and mix thoroughly over low heat. Check the seasoning, add kosher salt, and mix well. To serve, garnish with chopped chives.

HINTS FROM THE CHEF: The cream should be barely identifiable and entirely absorbed so that the pasta is light. Truffle juice and truffle oil can be obtained from Urbani Truffle, 425 West 25th Street, New York, NY 10011 or other specialty shops.

SERVES 6

PENNE ALL'ARRABBIATA

PRIMAVERA

4 tablespoons extra-virgin olive oil

$^1/_2$ teaspoon crushed dried red chili
    pepper

4 ounces pancetta, diced, optional

2 garlic cloves, peeled and crushed

$^1/_2$ cup white wine

one 28-ounce can peeled Italian
    tomatoes, crushed

salt and pepper to taste

1 pound penne rigate (imported)

1 tablespoon sweet butter (optional)

$^1/_2$ cup grated Parmesan cheese

$^1/_2$ cup grated pecorino cheese

3 fresh basil leaves, broken

1. In a heavy skillet, heat the oil over low heat and add the chili pepper, *pancetta*, if using, and the garlic cloves and brown lightly. Remove the garlic and *pancetta* from the pan and discard excess oil. Increase the heat and add the wine and crushed tomatoes. Season with salt and pepper to taste. After 10 minutes, turn heat down and simmer an additional 10 minutes to thicken the sauce.

2. In a pot of boiling lightly salted water, cook the *penne* until *al dente*, about 10 to 12 minutes. Drain.

3. Combine the *penne* with the sauce over low heat and add the remaining tablespoon of butter, if desired. Toss with the Parmesan and *pecorino* cheeses, add the basil leaves, and serve immediately.

HINT FROM THE CHEF: The best imported canned peeled Italian tomatoes are from San Marzano and consist of tomatoes, tomato juice and basil leaves. They are neither bitter nor sweet.

SERVES 6

This wonderfully spicy sauce arrabbiata, which means "furious" in Italian, is one of the best in town. It is topped with not only Parmesan cheese, but also pecorino, the Sardinian variety of sheep's milk cheese that is tangy and aged for grating. Actor Gene Wilder has been known to savor this aromatic dish.

*Inspired by a classical Venetian
dish, these roasted beet-filled ravioli
with light mushroom broth are a
titillating creation. Roasting the
beets brings out their sweetness,
and the sweet-sour combination of
the red onion marmalade topping
gives the dish its zest. The Sign of
the Dove, with its romantic decor
and skylights, has been called "the
Garden of Eden," a place where
the "food is as seductive as the
setting."*

BEET RAVIOLI WITH WILD MUSHROOM BROTH, RED ONION MARMALADE, AND GREENS

THE SIGN OF THE DOVE

1 pound whole fresh beets, with greens
    and beets washed and reserved

1 teaspoon olive oil

2 small red onions, unpeeled

6 garlic cloves, unpeeled

1/2 cup fresh orange juice

3 tablespoons red wine vinegar

zest of 1/2 lemon

zest of 1/2 navel orange

2 teaspoons honey

salt and freshly ground black pepper to
    taste

18 wonton skins

1 egg beaten with 1 tablespoon water

cornmeal for dredging

2 cups Light Chicken Stock (page 203)

1/2 pound mixed wild mushrooms,
    cleaned and sliced

2 shallots, peeled

2 garlic cloves, peeled

1 sprig thyme

6 tablespoons sweet butter

GARNISH
6 tablespoons sour cream

1. Preheat the oven to 350 degrees F.

2. Remove the beet greens and reserve. Rub the beets with the olive oil and
wrap them loosely in aluminum foil to prevent burning. Wrap 1 of the red
onions and the garlic cloves separately in foil. Roast all the vegetables in the
oven until soft. Cook the beets for 1¼ to 1½ hours and the onion and garlic
for about 45 minutes each.

3. Remove the skins from the beets, onion, and garlic. Place the vegetables in
a food processor and chop fine. Transfer the mixture to a wide-bottomed pan
and reduce over medium heat until almost dry, about 10 to 15 minutes. Add
the orange juice and 2 tablespoons of the vinegar and reduce again until
almost dry. Remove from the heat and add the lemon and orange zests,
honey, and salt and pepper to taste. Let the filling cool.

4. Divide the beet filling among the 18 wonton skins. Moisten the edges of
the skins with the beaten egg and fold each wonton into a triangle. Secure
the edges by pressing them together with your fingertips. Sprinkle the ravioli
with cornmeal to keep them separate and to prevent them from sticking.
Refrigerate until ready to use.

5. Make the broth: In a saucepan, combine the chicken stock with the mushrooms, shallots, garlic, and thyme. Bring to a boil, partially cover, and reduce the stock over medium heat by half. Remove the shallots and garlic and slowly whisk in 4 tablespoons of the butter. Season the broth with salt and pepper to taste and keep warm.

6. Make the onion marmalade: Peel the remaining onion and slice it into quarters. Cook it along with the remaining tablespoon of red wine vinegar and 1 tablespoon of butter over medium heat, stirring occasionally, until the onion softens as well.

7. Bring a large pot of water to a rapid boil, add the ravioli, and cook them for 1^{1}/$_{2}$ minutes. Drain well.

8. Melt the remaining 1 tablespoon of butter in a skillet and wilt the reserved beet greens. Divide the greens among 6 dinner plates. Arrange 3 ravioli around the greens on each plate and add the mushroom broth. Garnish each serving with sour cream and top with some of the onion marmalade.

HINT FROM THE CHEF: Instead of beet greens, you can also use kale, chard, or spinach greens. The filling freezes well and thus can be made in advance.

SERVES 6

This vegetable ravioli, a dish that originated in northern Piedmont, is delicately scented with saffron and oil from the truffles of Alba. While saffron, which is derived from the stigmas of the crocus, is admittedly precious, it enhances the dish with a special subtlety and color. The best saffron comes from Spain, and I recommend using threads rather than the powdered variety. Il Nido serves this ravioli with a variety of fillings, including lobster and buffalo ricotta.

VEGETABLE RAVIOLI WITH TRUFFLE OIL

IL NIDO

2 tablespoons dried porcini mushrooms

³/₄ cup water

FILLING

¹/₂ bunch arugula, washed and patted dry

4 sprigs parsley

4 basil leaves

6 leaves red or green romaine lettuce, washed and patted dry

6 leaves mâche, washed and patted dry

3 tablespoons buffalo ricotta

1 egg yolk

pinch of nutmeg

1¹/₂ tablespoons Parmesan cheese, finely grated

salt and freshly ground black pepper to taste

1 tablespoon olive oil

³/₄ POUND RAVIOLI DOUGH (page 201)

water for spraying

2 eggs, beaten

¹/₂ teaspoon saffron threads

1¹/₂ cups plus 1 tablespoon Light Chicken Stock (page 203)

SAUCE

1 tablespoon sweet butter

1 tablespoon truffle oil

GARNISH

4 tablespoons finely grated Parmesan cheese

1. Soak the dried *porcini* mushrooms in warm water for 1 hour. Reserve the soaking water for later use.

2. Make the filling: Place the arugula, parsley, basil leaves, romaine lettuce, *mâche*, and buffalo ricotta in a blender and purée until fine, but not liquefied. Place the mixture in a bowl, add the egg yolk, nutmeg, Parmesan, and salt and pepper to taste; combine well.

3. Fill the ravioli: Spray the pasta with water and then brush with the beaten eggs. Using a pastry bag or a teaspoon, place the filling on the dough 2 inches apart in horizontal rows so that when the ravioli is cut, each square will be 2 × 2 inches. Then place the remaining layer of pasta over the filling and press down to seal each ravioli. Dust well with semolina or all-purpose flour. Cut into 12 squares with a pastry cutter with a fluted edge, making sure that the edges are secured.

4. Cook the ravioli in a large pot of boiling salted water with the 1 tablespoon olive oil for 3 minutes. If cooking them in advance, shock the pasta in cold water after cooking to stop the cooking process.

5. Make the saffron water: In a saucepan, add the saffron threads to the $1^1/_2$ cups chicken stock and reduce to $^1/_2$ cup over medium heat.

6. Make the sauce: In a saucepan, melt the 1 tablespoon butter over low heat and add the $^1/_2$ cup saffron water, 2 tablespoons mushroom soaking water, and 1 tablespoon chicken stock. Cook for 2 minutes, stirring continuously. Add the truffle oil and remove from the heat.

7. To serve, place 6 ravioli on each plate, top with the sauce, and sprinkle with grated Parmesan cheese.

N O T E :   Fresh pasta for ravioli is available in rolls at specialty food stores.

S E R V E S   2

The luxuriously moist risotto, from the legendary Four Seasons, is one of the best around. Its subtlety is beguiling, and it can serve as the pièce de résistance of any Italian meal. This seasonal dish relies upon the availability of morels and asparagus, which are plentiful in the spring.

RISOTTO WITH OYSTER MUSHROOMS, MORELS, AND ASPARAGUS

THE FOUR SEASONS

4 or 5 asparagus spears

3 cups Light Chicken Stock (page 203), approximately, hot

5 tablespoons plus 2 teaspoons extra-virgin olive oil

1 cup morels (5 or 6), wiped clean and sliced crosswise

2 shallots, peeled and finely chopped

1 cup oyster mushrooms

kosher salt and freshly ground pepper to taste

1 cup superfine Arborio rice

4 tablespoons dry white wine, such as Chardonnay

1 garlic clove, peeled and finely diced

1 tablespoon sweet butter

1/2 jalapeño pepper, seeded and finely chopped

2 tablespoons finely chopped Italian parsley

2 teaspoons grated Parmesan cheese

1. Peel the asparagus spears and trim off 1 inch from the ends. In a saucepan, simmer the asparagus ends in the chicken stock for 30 minutes.

2. Cook the asparagus stalks (with the tips) in rapidly boiling salted water for 2 to 3 minutes, or until *al dente*. Chop into ¼-inch slices, saving the tips for garnish.

3. Heat 2 tablespoons of the olive oil in a saucepan and sauté the morels. Add half the chopped shallots and glaze lightly for approximately 2 minutes.

4. Wipe the oyster mushrooms with a cloth and remove the stems. When the morels and shallots are half cooked, add the oyster mushrooms and cook for 2 to 3 minutes. Season with salt and a pinch of pepper.

5. In a copper pan, sauté the remaining chopped shallots in 3 tablespoons of hot olive oil. If the rice is grainy, it should be cleaned prior to use (set a colander in a large bowl, place the rice in the colander, and run water through it). Add the rice to the pot and stir until it is warm and glazed. Add the wine, garlic, kosher salt, and ½ cup stock and continue stirring and pouring in the stock in ½ cup increments until all of it has been absorbed, approximately 15 minutes.

6. In another copper pan, combine the 2 teaspoons olive oil, butter, risotto, jalapeño pepper, and salt to taste. Add the oyster mushrooms, morels, and shallots and stir over low heat until heated through. Add the parsley and asparagus slices last or the vegetables will lose their flavor. Add the Parmesean cheese and asparagus tips and remove from the heat immediately.

7. Serve the risotto in large soup plates, leveling the mound on each plate with a wooden spoon.

HINTS FROM THE CHEF: Morels and oyster mushrooms should be wiped clean rather than washed as both types absorb water like a sponge. Stainless steel pots are not advisable for making risotto. It is best to use a copper pot as heat goes through it very quickly. If you want to make the risotto in advance, after Step 5, spread the risotto on a cookie sheet and level it with a wooden spoon. Cut it into squares like brownies so that the rice airs out. Cool in the refrigerator until ready to use.

SERVES 2

Risotto, made with the oval-shaped and short-grain Arborio rice that abounds in Italy's Piedmont region, is a legendary part of Italy's great culinary tradition. This creamy-textured Milanese risotto makes a formidable appetizer or main course. The delicate saffron flavor, reminiscent of tea, enhances the dish, while its vivid yellow threads brighten the risotto's appearance.

RISOTTO WITH SHRIMP, RADICCHIO, AND SAFFRON

IL NIDO

4 cups boiling Light Chicken Stock
    (page 203)
1 teaspoon saffron threads
1 large radicchio, *cut in half, with leaves separated*
2 tablespoons olive oil
¹/₂ onion, *peeled and finely chopped*

1¹/₂ cups superfine Arborio rice
1 cup plus 4 tablespoons dry white wine
2 tablespoons corn oil
6 large shrimp, *shelled, deveined, and cut into 1-inch pieces*

GARNISH
grated Parmesan cheese

1. Make the saffron water: In a small bowl, combine 4 tablespoons of the chicken stock and the saffron threads and let the mixture stand.

2. Heat a cast-iron skillet, add a drop of oil, 5 tablespoons of the chicken stock, and the *radicchio* and cook for 10 minutes, until the *radicchio* starts turning brown.

3. Meanwhile, in a large saucepan, heat the olive oil over high heat until hot. Add the onion and cook until translucent. Add the rice and stir slowly. Pour in the 1 cup wine until it is absorbed into the rice, stirring constantly with a wooden spoon. Gradually add 1¹/₂ cups chicken stock and continue stirring until the liquid is almost completely absorbed.

4. In a separate pan, heat the corn oil and sauté the shrimp for 2 to 3 minutes. Add the remaining 4 tablespoons wine, the braised *radicchio*, and ¹/₄ cup chicken stock, and cook over low heat for several minutes.

5. When the stock has been absorbed by the risotto mixture, stir in an additional 1¹/₂ cups stock and stir continuously. Once it is almost absorbed, taste the rice. If it is not cooked enough (although it should be served *al dente*), add additional stock as needed. The rice should not stick to the pan and there should be little stock apparent.

6. Five minutes before the risotto is ready and the stock has been absorbed, add the shrimp, saffron water, and *radicchio* to the pan and continue stirring until blended.

7. Serve immediately with grated Parmesan cheese.

SERVES 2

SPAGHETTINI WITH BROCCOLI RABE AND RADICCHIO

IL CANTINORI

2 pounds broccoli rabe, *trimmed and coarsely chopped*

1 head radicchio

¹/₄ cup olive oil

salt and freshly ground black pepper to

taste

4 garlic cloves, peeled

¹/₂ teaspoon crushed dried red pepper

flakes

³/₄ pound spaghettini

1. Preheat the oven to 400 degrees F.

2. Wash the *broccoli rabe* and *radicchio* and pat dry. Cut the *radicchio* into shreds and place in a roasting pan or cast-iron skillet with 2 tablespoons of the olive oil. Add salt and pepper to taste. Brown in the oven for about 7 minutes.

3. Heat the remaining olive oil in a deep saucepan and brown the garlic. Add the *broccoli rabe*, salt, and red pepper flakes and cook until the *broccoli rabe* is reduced in size by half. Add the browned *radicchio* and combine thoroughly.

4. Meanwhile, cook the spaghettini in a pot of rapidly boiling salted water for 5 to 7 minutes, or until *al dente*. Drain the spaghettini, reserving about ¹/₄ cup of the pasta water.

5. Add the pasta and pasta water to the broccoli mixture, sprinkle with additional olive oil as desired, and serve at once.

SERVES 4

The intoxicating aroma of garlic is one of the hallmarks of a great Italian meal, and garlic heightens the tartness of radicchio and broccoli rabe. Broccoli rabe is plentiful in the mountainous region of Abruzzi, where it thrives in the cool climate both in autumn and winter. Il Cantinori pioneered the cooking of broccoli rabe, otherwise known as broccoli di rape in New York City, and it remains a mainstay of the premier Italian restaurants.

MEAT AND FOWL

This lamb and duck cassoulet is a classic dish of Gascony and Languedoc in southwestern France. It requires slow, gentle cooking of the meat and lentils to bring out their rich flavor. This cooking style was originally brought to France in the Middle Ages by Eastern European Jews who used it to prepare cholent *for the Sabbath observance.*

LAMB AND DUCK CASSOULET WITH LENTILS

CAFE DES ARTISTES

1 pound lentils, sorted and rinsed

4 cups cold water

1 pound boneless lamb, cut into medium pieces

salt and freshly ground black pepper to taste

3 tablespoons olive oil

1 pound slab bacon, cut into 1-inch cubes

1¹/₂ tablespoons finely chopped garlic

2 ripe tomatoes, peeled, seeded, and coarsely chopped

¹/₂ cup tomato purée (or 1 tablespoon tomato paste)

4 whole cloves

4 bay leaves

1 onion, peeled and cut in half crosswise

2 teaspoons dried thyme, crushed

8 cups Dark Chicken Stock (page 203) or duck stock

³/₄ pound garlic sausage, blanched and cut into ¹/₂-inch slices

5 legs (with thighs) of boneless Duck Confit, leg and thigh meat pulled from the bones (page 197)

1 cup bread crumbs

4 tablespoons chopped fresh parsley

4 tablespoons rendered duck fat, lard, or butter, melted

GARNISH

6 sprigs Italian parsley

1. Place the lentils in a large soup pot, cover with the cold water, and let them soak for 8 hours or overnight. Drain. Cover again with water and bring them to a quick boil. Cook over medium-high heat until tender, approximately 10 to 12 minutes. Drain.

2. Season the lamb with salt and pepper to taste. Heat the oil in a large saucepan and when very hot, add the lamb. Sear until nicely browned all over, about 3 minutes. Discard the excess oil.

3. Add the bacon to the pan and brown, stirring well. Add the chopped garlic to the pan and cook an additional 5 minutes. Stir in the tomatoes and tomato purée.

4. Use the cloves to fasten a whole bay leaf to each onion half. Add the onions with the thyme and half the stock to the pan and bring to a boil. Reduce heat to a simmer and braise, partially covered, for 45 minutes, skimming off the scum from time to time. Stir in the cooked lentils and the remaining stock and continue cooking, uncovered, for 30 minutes. Cover and let sit for 30 minutes. Remove the onion halves and discard.

5. Preheat the oven to 400 degrees F.

6. Add the sausage and duck confit to the pan and cook over medium heat an additional 10 minutes. Add salt and pepper to taste.

7. In a bowl, toss together the bread crumbs and parsley. Combine well with the rendered duck fat.

8. To serve, ladle the cassoulet into shallow, oval, ovenproof earthenware dishes, approximately 6 inches long, $3^{1}/_{2}$ inches wide, and $1^{1}/_{2}$ inches deep. Alternatively, place in one large casserole. Fill the dishes. Cover the top of each serving with the bread crumb and parsley mixture and bake in the oven until golden brown and crusty, approximately 3 to 4 minutes. Garnish with fresh parsley and serve immediately.

SERVES 8

Whimsical murals of frolicking nymphs adorn the walls of Café des Artistes, a salon de thé reminiscent of a turn of the century Budapest café.

*A savory tomato sauce of garlic,
artichokes, and porcini mushrooms
characterizes this flavorful chicken
cacciatore. Giambelli's classic
"hunter-style" chicken will please
even the most demanding palate.*

CHICKEN CACCIATORE

GIAMBELLI 50

1 ounce dried porcini *mushrooms*

*two 3-pound chickens, skinned, boned,
    and cut into eighths*

*salt and freshly ground black pepper to
    taste*

all-purpose flour for dusting

1 cup corn or vegetable oil

1 sprig rosemary

2 teaspoons minced shallot

2 teaspoons chopped garlic

20 fresh artichoke hearts, halved

2 cups sliced domestic mushrooms

1 tablespoon sweet butter

1 cup dry white wine

*2 cups tomato sauce (follow the sauce
    recipe for Penne All'Arrabiata, page
    77)*

2 cups Light Chicken Stock (page 203)

3 basil leaves, finely chopped

1. Rinse the *porcini* mushrooms and soak in warm water to cover for 30 minutes. Drain off all but 2 tablespoons of the water. Coarsely chop the mushrooms.

2. Cut the chicken into 1-inch pieces. Season with salt and pepper and lightly dust with flour. Heat the oil in a large saucepan until very hot and brown the chicken on both sides until golden, approximately 5 minutes. Remove from the heat and drain the excess oil, leaving the chicken in the pan.

3. Add the rosemary, chopped mushrooms, shallot, garlic, artichoke hearts, sliced mushrooms, and butter to the pan. Cook until the shallots are golden, then deglaze the pan with white wine and cook until the wine evaporates. Add the tomato sauce and chicken stock and simmer over low heat until the sauce thickens and the chicken is tender. Adjust the salt and pepper to taste. Add the basil, remove the rosemary, and serve.

SERVES 4

BARBECUED CHICKEN WITH SCALLIONS

C A N T O N

*one 3-pound chicken, skinned, boned,
and the meat cut into cubes*

5 tablespoons sherry or scotch whiskey

2 tablespoons peanut oil or vegetable oil

one 1-inch piece of ginger with peel

2 garlic cloves, peeled

1/4 teaspoon salt

1 scallion, cut into 1-inch pieces

2 tablespoons oyster sauce

pinch of white pepper

This intensely flavored chicken is a masterpiece of refined Chinese cuisine. Oyster sauce, a typical basting ingredient in Cantonese cooking, adds a subtle flavor and the stir-fried scallions lend a zesty sweetness.

1. Marinate the chicken in 3 tablespoons of the sherry or whiskey for 30 minutes.

2. Heat a wok until hot and add the peanut oil, covering the sides and bottom. Brown the ginger and garlic, stirring continuously with metal tongs, and tipping the wok so that the sides get direct heat.

3. Add the chicken to the wok, press down with the metal tongs, and pan-fry until browned. Do not stir. When browned, press down hard so that you can turn the chicken as if in one piece and brown the other side approximately 10 minutes. Cover and continue cooking for 1 or 2 minutes over lower heat.

4. Drain the oil from the wok, if necessary. Add the salt, scallion, and 2 remaining tablespoons sherry or whiskey and stir-fry. Add the oyster sauce and a pinch of white pepper and stir-fry until well mixed.

5. Serve immediately with steamed white rice.

N O T E :   Oyster sauce is available at Oriental markets.

S E R V E S 4

CHICKEN AND DUCK PIE WITH ASPARAGUS, WILD MUSHROOMS, AND PEAS

PARK AVENUE CAFE

Lusty flavors characterize this aromatic dish rimmed with a poppy seed border. A new twist on the classic American chicken pot pie, this version is permeated with such irresistible delicacies as shiitake mushrooms, duck confit, and pearl onions.

This sumptuous indulgence, an example of Chef David Burke's fanciful and inspired cooking, presents a challenge to gastronomic enthusiasts but is well worth the effort.

1 pound boneless skinless chicken thighs, plus 6 whole drumsticks with skin

6 tablespoons plus 2 cups whole wheat flour for dredging

salt and freshly ground white pepper to taste

3 tablespoons Clarified Butter (page 196), or ¹/₄ cup olive oil

1 tablespoon sweet butter

³/₄ pound shiitake mushrooms, diced

6 stalks celery, cut into 1-inch pieces

6 carrots, peeled and cut on the diagonal

3 medium turnips, peeled and diced

2¹/₂ quarts Dark Chicken Stock (page 203)

8 tablespoons finely chopped fresh herbs:

  2 tablespoons tarragon

  2 tablespoons thyme

  2 tablespoons chives

  2 tablespoons Italian parsley

¹/₂ pound Duck Confit (page 197), removed from the bone

³/₄ pound Parker House Rolls (page 200)

EGG WASH

1 egg

2 tablespoons water

2 tablespoons black poppy seeds

1 cup fresh peas, shelled

18 asparagus spears and tips, cut in half lengthwise and then on the diagonal into 1-inch pieces

18 pearl onions, peeled

GARNISH

6 bay leaves

1. Preheat the oven to 400 degrees F.

2. Cut the skinless chicken thighs into large 1-inch chunks. Chop 1 inch of the bone off one end of each drumstick and ¹/₂ inch off the other end. Reserve. Dredge the thigh meat with the whole wheat flour seasoned with salt and white pepper. Place the chicken in a strainer and shake to remove excess flour.

(recipe continues on next page)

3. In a large *rondot* or stockpot, melt 2 tablespoons of the clarified butter until the pan is very hot and brown the thigh meat until crispy and golden brown on both sides. Remove the thigh meat from the pot, discarding the excess butter. Add 1 tablespoon of sweet butter and when it starts bubbling add the mushrooms, and cook until you start to smell their nutty essence. Remove half and reserve for garnish. Lower the heat and add the celery, carrots, and turnips and combine with the butter. Cover and sweat over lower heat until translucent, approximately 10 minutes. Return the thigh meat to the pot and sprinkle with the 6 tablespoons whole wheat flour. Incorporate by stirring until the juices have been absorbed.

4. In a separate pan, simmer 6 cups of the chicken stock with 4 tablespoons of the herbs for approximately 10 minutes. Strain through a fine *chinois* or strainer. Add the strained stock to the large stockpot and cook for 25 to 30 minutes, or until the sauce coats the back of a spoon and the thigh meat is tender.

5. In a skillet, heat 1 tablespoon clarified butter and sear the drumsticks. Add 4 cups chicken stock, then braise the drumsticks for 30 minutes, or until the meat is tender.

6. Divide equal amounts of the filling among 6 crocks, reserving 1 cup of the sauce for the vegetable garnish. Pull the duck confit off the bone and divide among the crocks. Roll the Parker House dough into logs $^1/_2$ inch in diameter and cut into $^1/_2$-inch cylindrical pieces. Line the rim of each crock with dough pieces placed vertically abutting one another, pressing against the sides.

7. Make the egg wash: Beat the egg with the water. Lightly brush the dough with the egg wash. Sprinkle poppy seeds over the dough. Place the crocks in a warm spot to proof the dough for thirty minutes. Place 1 chicken drumstick vertically into the center of each crock. Transfer the crocks to the oven and bake for 10 to 12 minutes, or until the dough is golden brown.

8. While the dough is baking, blanch the peas, asparagus, and pearl onions. Pour the reserved cup of sauce into a saucepan and add the vegetables, *shiitake* mushrooms, and the remaining chopped herbs. Simmer for 5 minutes.

9. To serve, remove the crocks from the oven and carefully distribute the vegetables and sauce evenly among the crocks. Garnish each drumstick with a bay leaf.

SERVES 6

CHICKEN SCARPARIELLO

NICOLA'S

two 1¹/₂-pound chickens

1 cup flour

¹/₂ cup plus 2 tablespoons soybean oil

4 tablespoons finely chopped garlic

4 tablespoons fresh rosemary leaves

1 cup dry white wine

1 tablespoon lemon juice

1 cup Brown Veal Stock (page 207)

1 cup Light Chicken Stock (page 203)

sea salt and freshly ground pepper to
     taste

2 tablespoons chopped Italian parsley

"Scarpariello," *Italian for
shoemaker's style, is a rustic
Neapolitan dish popular
throughout Italy. Enriched with
both veal and chicken stocks, this
robustly flavored chicken, scented
with garlic and rosemary, makes an
irresistibly delightful, fragrant meal.*

1. Remove all the chicken meat from the bones except on the wings and legs. Cut all the chicken meat into 2-inch pieces and lightly flour. Reserve the wings and legs for other uses.

2. In a large skillet, heat the oil until it smokes. Add the chicken and sauté until golden brown on both sides. Discard the excess oil.

3. Add the garlic, rosemary, and wine to the pan. Cover and braise slowly over medium heat until the wine is reduced by half. Add the lemon juice, veal stock, chicken stock, salt and pepper to taste, and parsley and cook until the sauce thickens. Serve immediately.

SERVES 4

Inspired by the classic pot au feu,
*this robust chicken creation remains
one of La Grenouille's signature
dishes. Served with flavorful
sculptured vegetables simmered in
chicken broth and a piquant sauce
made with fresh horseradish strips,
the poached chicken provides a
nourishing meal on a cold winter
evening.*

POACHED CHICKEN WITH COARSE SALT IN HORSERADISH SAUCE

LA GRENOUILLE

3 chickens, 2^1/$_2$ pounds each

3 quarts Light Chicken Stock
  (page 203)

2 leeks, trimmed

10 carrots, peeled

2 stalks celery, cut in half

2 onions, peeled and sliced

2 garlic cloves, peeled and smashed

2 bay leaves

1 branch thyme

1 bunch parsley

SAUCE

3 tablespoons sweet butter

2 tablespoons flour

10 large domestic mushrooms, thinly
  sliced

1 stalk celery, diced

^{1}/$_2$ large onion, peeled and diced

2 cups heavy cream

salt and white pepper to taste

2 whole horseradish roots

1 teaspoon freshly squeezed lemon juice

VEGETABLES

10 medium turnips, peeled

4 stalks celery, strings removed, cut into
  3 sections

5 leeks, white part and 1 inch green

16 baby carrots, peeled, with ^{1}/$_4$-inch of
  stem remaining

12 small white-skinned potatoes (or 6
  Idaho), peeled

1 green cabbage, cut in half

^{1}/$_2$ bunch parsley, stemmed and chopped

gherkins, optional

coarse salt, to taste

1. Remove the excess fat from the chicken cavities, and truss by tying with
string at both ends, making sure to tie in the wings.

2. Bring the chicken stock to a boil in a large pot. Cut the trimmed leeks in
half lengthwise and rinse well. Clean the other vegetables. In a large soup
pot, place the chickens vertically, add leeks, carrots, celery, onions, garlic
cloves, bay leaves, thyme, and parsley and cover with the boiling chicken
stock. Bring to a boil again over medium heat, skimming off the scum as it
rises to the top. Partially cover the pot with the lid (three-quarters of the
pot should be covered). Poach the chickens over low heat until tender,
approximately 40 minutes, turning the chickens half way through the
cooking time. Remove the chickens from the pot and place them on a
plate covered with damp towels (this will help keep the chickens moist).
Pour the stock through a strainer lined with cheesecloth into another

pan and reserve for cooking the sauce and the vegetables. Refrigerate until ready to use.

3. Make the *sauce suprême:* Melt 2 tablespoons of the butter in a large saucepan over a low heat. When it bubbles, add the flour, whisking constantly to make a light *roux.* Take care not to let it brown. Cook for a few minutes. Immediately whisk in 1^1/$_2$ quarts of the chicken stock and allow to simmer. Melt the additional tablespoon of butter in another saucepan, adding the mushrooms, celery, and onion. Simmer these vegetables for approximately 5 minutes. Add these vegetables to the sauce made from the stock and the *roux.* Whisk in the cream, salt, and white pepper. Bring the sauce to a boil again, then reduce the heat to a simmer for 10 minutes. Strain the *sauce suprême* into a large bowl.

4. Make the horseradish sauce: Peel the horseradish roots and grate them with the large end of a hand grater or the grater attachment of a food processor. Add the grated horseradish root to the hot *sauce suprême.* Cover with plastic wrap and let infuse for 15 minutes. Mix the sauce with a hand blender and then strain through a fine *chinois,* pressing hard to squeeze the horseradish dry. Season to taste with salt, white pepper, and a dash of lemon juice. Reheat when ready to serve.

5. Prepare the garnish: Carve the turnips, celery, leeks, carrots, and potatoes into 1^1/$_2$-inch oval shapes. Place all the vegetables (except the potatoes) in a large pot with the remaining chicken stock and cook over medium heat until tender. Drain and then remove the vegetables and keep warm, reserving the stock in the pan. Boil the potatoes in the stock until tender. Remove the potatoes, reserve the stock, and keep the potatoes warm.

6. Blanch the cabbage in a pot of rapidly boiling water for approximately 5 minutes. Drain, then cook in the reserved chicken stock for approximately 15 minutes.

7. To serve, cut the chicken into individual portions and arrange on plates. Surround the chicken with the vegetables and cabbage. Spoon the horseradish sauce over all and sprinkle a pinch of coarse salt onto each piece of chicken. Garnish with chopped parsley. Pass a bowl of coarse salt and gherkins.

SERVES 6

DUCK IN SPICY SAUCE

TSE YANG

6 boneless duck breasts, fat and skin
    removed

1 egg white

1 teaspoon dry cornstarch

8 Chinese dried black mushrooms

2 cups soybean oil

1 cup cubed green bell pepper

1 cup cubed red bell pepper

1 teaspoon chopped garlic

$1/2$ carrot, peeled and thinly sliced

2 tablespoons peeled, shredded ginger

1 teaspoon chili sauce

3 tablespoons bamboo shoots, shredded
    into 1-inch pieces

2 scallions, cut into 2-inch pieces

1. Slice the duck breasts into thin 2-inch-long pieces and marinate in a mixture of egg white and cornstarch for 30 minutes.

2. Pour boiling water over the dried mushrooms and soak for 30 minutes. Drain and dice.

3. In a very large wok, heat the soybean oil until very hot. Add the duck and stir-fry vigorously for 45 seconds, until just cooked through. Remove the duck and drain well. Remove all but 1 tablespoon of the oil from the wok.

4. Add the green and red bell peppers, garlic, carrot, ginger, chili sauce, bamboo shoots, mushrooms, and scallions to the wok and stir-fry until the vegetables are tender and crisp. Return the duck to the wok and stir-fry quickly to heat through. Serve immediately with steamed rice.

HINT FROM THE CHEF: The key to this dish is marinating the duck meat in the egg white, which tenderizes it.

SERVES 4

This tender rendition of duck, with crunchy red and green peppers, is a satisfying way to enjoy duck without worrying about the fat. Shredded ginger, used widely in Chinese cooking, adds a delightful pungency to this dish.

    Tse Yang, with restaurants worldwide, is devoted primarily to the cuisine of Beijing province, where peppers and other vegetables abound.

*Thai flavors continue to influence
American cooking, and Tommy
Tang was one of the first to
popularize Thai cuisine in the
United States. This classic Thai
duck with its crispy lacquered
coating is artfully presented, as are
many Thai culinary creations.
Plums, ginger, and honey
distinguish the savory sauce.*

DUCK WITH HONEY-GINGER SAUCE

TOMMY TANG'S

MARINADE
1/2 cup light soy sauce
1/2 cup onion, peeled and cut into large
   chunks
1/4 cup fresh ginger, peeled and chopped
1 cup water

two 3-pound Long Island ducklings
   (6 pounds duck in all)

3 cups vegetable oil

HONEY-GINGER SAUCE
1 cup honey
1 cup plus 2 tablespoons water
1/4 cup plum sauce

1/4 cup soy sauce
4 tablespoons fresh ginger, peeled and
   sliced
1 teaspoon all-purpose flour
1/4 teaspoon black pepper
1/4 teaspoon white pepper
1 teaspoon chili powder
1 teaspoon garlic powder
4 stems cilantro, leaves only, chopped
1 large zucchini, cut into quarters
   lengthwise

GARNISH
4 cilantro sprigs
1 daikon, *peeled and grated*
1 carrot, *peeled and grated*

1. Make the marinade: Combine the light soy sauce, onion, and ginger and grind well in a food processor. Add the water and blend well. In a bowl, pour the marinade over the ducks, cover the bowl, and marinate overnight in the refrigerator.

2. Preheat the oven to 350 degrees F. Remove the ducks to a roasting pan and strain the marinade.

3. Pour 1 cup of the strained marinade over the ducks and roast for 1 1/2 hours, basting every 15 minutes. Let cool.

4. Remove the backbones from the ducks. In a large saucepan, heat the vegetable oil to 350 degrees F. and deep-fry the ducks (one at a time) until the skin is crispy, approximately 3 to 5 minutes. Drain the ducks on paper towels.

5. Make the sauce: Combine the honey, 1 cup water, plum sauce, soy sauce, and ginger in a saucepan and bring to a boil over high heat. Mix together the flour and 2 tablespoons water, and add to the sauce mixture. Stir the mixture with a wooden spoon, reduce the heat, and simmer until syrupy, approximately 20 minutes.

6. In a small bowl, combine the black and white pepper, chili powder, garlic powder, and cilantro. Brush the zucchini with oil and sprinkle with the pepper seasoning. Place on a hot grill or under a preheated broiler and cook until tender, approximately 5 minutes.

7. To serve, remove the duck meat from the bones and slice. Divide the slices equally among dinner plates and arrange artfully, fanning out the slices. Spoon the honey-ginger sauce around the plates. Place a piece of grilled zucchini next to the duck. Garnish each serving with a sprig of cilantro, and stack grated *daikon* and carrot on the side.

S E R V E S 4

RACK OF LAMB ROMAN STYLE

IL MULINO

SAUCE

1 pound lamb bones, cut into small
   pieces

1/2 cup plus 2 tablespoons olive oil

1 cup dry sherry

1 cup balsamic vinegar

4 garlic cloves, peeled and crushed

1 tablespoon fresh rosemary

1 rack of lamb (8 ribs)

sea salt and freshly ground black pepper
   to taste

2 tablespoons olive oil

3 tablespoons Dijon mustard

2 tablespoons bread crumbs

4 slices smoked bacon

3 garlic cloves, peeled and crushed

1 Idaho potato, peeled and cut into 1/2-
   inch cubes

2 tablespoons sweet butter

1 tablespoon fresh rosemary, finely
   chopped

*In rack of lamb Roman style,
bacon is used to flavor the meat
during cooking. This technique is
an Italian tradition as old as the
Roman Empire.*

*The rosemary-infused lamb
sauce, heightened in complexity by
a reduction of sherry and balsamic
vinegar, adds a delicacy of flavor,
making this a most memorable
roast.*

1. Make the sauce: In a large saucepan, cook the lamb bones in 1/2 cup of very hot olive oil until browned. Add the sherry and cook until the liquor evaporates. Add the balsamic vinegar and deglaze the pan. In another pan, heat 2 tablespoons of the olive oil until very hot and brown 4 garlic cloves. Add the browned garlic and the rosemary to the sauce. Simmer for 10 minutes. Strain the sauce into another pan and cook it until reduced by half, approximately 20 minutes. Reheat when ready to serve.

2. Preheat the oven to 450 degrees F.

3. Season the rack of lamb all over with salt and pepper. In a skillet, sear the lamb in hot olive oil. Coat with Dijon mustard and bread crumbs and roast in the oven for 15 minutes. Place the bacon along the inside bones of the lamb rack and return to the oven for 15 minutes. Add 2 garlic cloves and spoon pan juices over the lamb while it cooks. Discard the bacon and skim the fat from the pan juices. Place the meat in a hot pan with the pan juices.

4. Make the potatoes: Partially cook the potato cubes in rapidly boiling water for 3 to 4 minutes. Drain. In a saucepan, melt the butter and add the potatoes, rosemary, remaining garlic clove, and salt and pepper to taste and cook until browned.

5. To serve, slice the rack of lamb and arrange on dinner plates. Generously pour sauce onto each plate and serve with the browned potatoes.

SERVES 2

The namesake of Lespinasse, Madame Julie Lespinasse, established a salon de thé during the seventeenth century, which became a gathering place for the rich and famous and a precursor to what we know as a restaurant today. The food at Lespinasse is consistent with the composed formality of its palatial setting.

This lamb chop with eggplant tart is a complex rendering of exotic flavors influenced by Indian and Thai cuisines. Such combinations distinguish the cuisine of Singapore-born chef Gray Kunz.

LAMB CHOP WITH EGGPLANT TART WITH CURRY-CARROT JUICE SAUCE

LESPINASSE

EGGPLANT TARTS

3 eggplants

¹/₂ cup extra-virgin olive oil

4 garlic cloves, peeled and chopped

3 tomatoes, peeled and diced

2 bay leaves

1 onion, peeled and sliced

¹/₂ teaspoon curry powder

1 tablespoon vinegar

salt and pepper to taste

1 tablespoon chopped parsley

1 tablespoon chopped chives

1 tablespoon chopped basil

CURRY-CARROT JUICE
SAUCE

1 cup carrot juice

1 teaspoon finely chopped fresh ginger

2 tablespoons sweet butter, cut into bits

salt and cayenne pepper to taste

LAMB CHOPS

four 6-ounce triple lamb chops, frenched with one bone only, and lightly pounded

sea salt to taste

2 tablespoons olive or corn oil

2 tablespoons sweet butter

¹/₄ teaspoon brown mustard seeds

¹/₂ teaspoon coriander seeds

¹/₄ teaspoon ground cumin

¹/₄ teaspoon curry powder

¹/₄ cup bread crumbs

¹/₄ cup toasted pine nuts, chopped

1 tablespoon chopped mint

GARNISH

1 tablespoon chopped chives

pink peppercorns

curry powder

¹/₂ bunch thyme sprigs

1. Make the eggplant tarts: Preheat the oven to 350 degrees F. Cut 2 of the eggplants in half lengthwise; brush the flesh with olive oil. Roast in the oven until tender. Scoop out the flesh and purée it in a blender or by hand until smooth. Pass the purée through a fine sieve, pressing on it, into a bowl.

2. Cut the remaining eggplant lengthwise into thin slices. Heat 1 tablespoon of olive oil in a large skillet, add the eggplant slices, and sauté until golden on both sides. Remove the slices from the pan and set aside on a cloth towel so that the excess oil is absorbed.

3. In the same skillet, sauté the garlic until golden brown. Add the diced tomatoes and bay leaves, and simmer until the tomatoes start disintegrating.

4. In another pan, sauté the sliced onion in 1 tablespoon of olive oil over high heat until dark brown. Add the curry powder, cook for 1 minute, and then deglaze the pan with the vinegar. Season with salt and pepper to taste.

5. In a bowl, mix the eggplant purée with the sautéed tomatoes and the onions. Add the chopped herbs and season with salt and pepper to taste.

6. Preheat the oven to 250 degrees F. Line four 5-inch metal rings with the eggplant slices so that the slices emanate from the center of the mold like spokes. Then fill the molds three-quarters full with the seasoned eggplant purée and fold the eggplant slices back toward the center, firmly pressing closed. Heat the eggplant tarts in the oven for 8 to 10 minutes, until golden brown.

7. Make the curry-carrot juice sauce: Heat the carrot juice in a saucepan over medium heat until reduced by half. Add the chopped ginger and simmer for 4 to 5 minutes. Strain the carrot juice through a fine sieve into a pan and slowly swirl in the butter, bit by bit. Season with salt and cayenne pepper to taste. Cover and keep warm.

8. Prepare the lamb chops: Season the lamb chops with the salt and sauté in the olive oil to desired doneness. Add butter to the pan and spoon the juices over the top of the lamb chops. Preheat the broiler. In a small bowl, mix the brown mustard seeds, coriander seeds, cumin, curry powder, bread crumbs, pine nuts, and mint. Carefully top each lamb chop with the spice mixture, making sure the topping is set firmly like a dome. Brown the lamb chops under the preheated broiler until the topping becomes golden.

9. To serve, place 1 eggplant tart in the center of each dinner plate and remove the ring. Place a lamb chop on top of each tart and surround with the warm sauce. Garnish the sauce with chopped chives, pink peppercorns, and sprinkle with curry powder. Place a thyme sprig in each eggplant tart.

SERVES 4

*La Caravelle, named after the type
of ship on which Columbus sailed,
offers such riveting classics as this
filet mignon in Merlot sauce. The
smooth Merlot sauce with crunchy
apple and mushroom duxelles
flecked with truffles exemplifies La
Caravelle's classic cooking, but with
a new twist. The crisp potato
rosette, perched on top of the
luscious filet, makes a stunning
presentation.*

BLACK ANGUS FILET MIGNON IN MERLOT SAUCE

LA CARAVELLE

MERLOT SAUCE
1 tablespoon chopped peeled shallot
4 tablespoons cold sweet butter
1 teaspoon cracked black pepper
1 cup Merlot (or other good red wine)
1 tablespoon Port wine
1 cup Brown Veal Stock (page 207)
salt and freshly ground black pepper to
   taste

1 apple, peeled, cored, and diced
4 white mushrooms, stemmed and diced

*DUXELLES (MUSHROOM
   PUREE)*
2 tablespoons sweet butter
2 tablespoons peeled chopped shallots

$^1/_2$ pound white mushrooms, stemmed
   and finely chopped
1 teaspoon heavy cream
salt and pepper to taste
1 tablespoon chopped black truffle

4 Idaho potatoes
$^1/_4$ cup Clarified Butter (page 196)
4 Black Angus filets mignons, 8 ounces
   each
1 teaspoon butter
1 tablespoon vegetable oil

GARNISH
4 sprigs chervil or watercress

1. Make the Merlot sauce: Sweat the shallot in 1 tablespoon of butter over low heat with the cracked pepper until the shallot is translucent; add the Merlot and Port and reduce by two-thirds. Add the veal stock and reduce for approximately 10 minutes to create a thick sauce. Season with salt and pepper to taste. Cut 2 tablespoons of the cold butter into bits and whisk into the sauce. Strain the sauce through a fine-mesh strainer into a clean saucepan. Reheat when ready to serve.

2. In a separate pan, melt the remaining 1 tablespoon of butter over low heat, add the diced apples and mushrooms, and cook until soft. Add the apple-mushroom mixture to the Merlot sauce.

3. Make the duxelles: In a saucepan, melt the butter and sweat the shallot until translucent. Add the mushrooms and cook slowly for approximately 20 minutes, until they exude their liquid. Add the heavy cream and salt and pepper to taste. Boil down rapidly, until the liquid is evaporated. Add the truffle and remove from the heat.

4. Make the potato rosettes: Peel the potatoes and slice into very thin rounds. On four 3-inch rounds of parchment or wax paper, overlap the potato slices to make 4 rosettes, using the slices from 1 potato for each rosette. Melt 1 tablespoon of the clarified butter in a sauté pan over medium heat, then slide the potato rosette into the pan, parchment side up. Remove parchment paper and cook for about 3 to 5 minutes on each side, or until golden brown. Repeat the cooking procedure for the 3 remaining rosettes. When ready to serve, reheat in a preheated 350 degree F. oven for a few minutes.

5. Cook the filets mignons: Preheat the oven to 400 degrees F. Season the filets with salt and pepper to taste. Heat the butter and oil in an ovenproof skillet over high heat and add the filets. Brown on both sides, turning once. Transfer the skillet to the oven until the beef reaches the desired doneness.

6. To assemble: Place a 3-inch ring mold on each dinner plate and fill to the rim with the duxelles. Gently remove the mold, then place a filet mignon on top of the duxelles. Place a potato rosette on top of each filet, then pour the sauce generously around the meat. Garnish with chervil or watercress sprig.

HINT FROM THE CHEF: Truffles should not be overcooked or they will lose their flavor.

SERVES 4

*Le Perigord is named after the
region in southwest France
renowned for its abundance of
truffles, game, goose, and* foie
gras. *This richly flavored pheasant
with mushroom* fumet *exemplifies
Chef Antoine Bouterin's talent for
combining classical and* nouvelle
cuisines.

PHEASANT WITH GREEN CABBAGE CHIFFONNADE AND FUMET OF WILD MUSHROOMS

LE PERIGORD

1 medium cabbage

6 juniper berries, chopped

salt and freshly ground black pepper to
   taste

3 teaspoons olive oil

one 4- to 5-pound pheasant

3 carrots, peeled

6 shallots, peeled and chopped

1 teaspoon flour

1 cup dry white wine

1 cup Light Chicken Stock (page 203)

$1^{1}/_{2}$ tablespoons sweet butter, softened

MUSHROOM SAUCE

1 pound dried wild mushrooms

2 cups warm water

2 cups warm Light Chicken Stock
   (page 203)

4 tablespoons peanut oil

1 onion, peeled and coarsely chopped

1 carrot, peeled

GARNISH

2 tablespoons finely chopped chives or
   parsley

12 sage leaves

1. Reserving 4 outer leaves, cut the cabbage in half and finely slice. Place the sliced cabbage and 4 chopped juniper berries in rapidly boiling salted water. Season with salt, pepper, and a splash of olive oil, and steam the cabbage for 8 minutes, until *al dente.* Drain and reserve. (The juniper berries remain in the cabbage.)

2. Clean the pheasant well and carve into pieces. Debone the breasts, salt them lightly, pat with the remaining olive oil, and reserve.

3. Preheat the oven to 375 degrees F.

4. In a pan, roast the remaining pheasant parts with 1 sliced carrot and the shallots for 40 minutes. Remove the pheasant parts and excess oil from the pan, leaving just the juices, and quickly whisk in the flour. Add the white wine and chicken stock and reduce by half until the sauce reaches a velvety consistency, approximately 15 to 20 minutes. Add the remaining juniper berries and cook for 2 additional minutes. Strain the sauce into another pan, then whisk in the butter. Reheat when ready to serve.

5. Make the mushroom sauce: Wipe the mushrooms clean and soak in the warm water and chicken stock for 2 to 3 hours. In a large saucepan, heat 2 tablespoons of peanut oil. Add the onion and 1 carrot and cook until the onion is translucent. Add the mushroom and stock mixture and cook uncovered over medium heat for 1 hour. Strain through a fine-mesh sieve or *chinois* into another pan and add the sauce from step 4. Cook over medium heat for 15 to 20 minutes then set aside. Reheat when ready to serve.

6. Julienne the remaining carrots and steam in rapidly boiling water for 10 minutes. Drain.

7. Preheat the broiler. Heat the remaining peanut oil in a large saucepan. Add the pheasant breast filets and brown on both sides. Remove the breasts from the pan and slice them in half lengthwise. Cut them again into 3 or 4 thin slices. Broil the pheasant slices until they are cooked throughout, approximately 5 minutes.

8. To serve, garnish each plate with a reserved cabbage leaf. In the center of the plate, spoon a mound of cabbage slices, and arrange pheasant slices on top of the cabbage like spokes in a wheel. Spoon the reserved sauce over and around the pheasant slices. Sprinkle with the julienned carrots and season with freshly ground pepper. Garnish with chives or parsley and top each portion with 3 sage leaves.

SERVES 4

In this inventive dish, Larry
Forgione, one of America's great
master chefs, utilizes native
American game and indigenous
wild rice. Enriched with chicken
stock and pecans, the wild rice
sauce, with its nutty flavor,
provides the perfect accompaniment
to the roast pheasant. Committed
to using only the finest American
ingredients, Forgione has made a
statement about our country's
gastronomic bounty.

ROAST PHEASANT WITH WILD RICE SAUCE AND GLAZED PEARL ONIONS

AN AMERICAN PLACE

two 2¹/₂-pound pheasants

6 tablespoons olive oil

kosher salt and freshly ground black
    pepper

1 onion, peeled and sliced

1 garlic clove, peeled and crushed

5 cups Light Chicken Stock (page 203)

1 cup heavy cream

2 teaspoons cornstarch

¹/₂ cup wild rice

¹/₂ pound chanterelle mushrooms,
    chopped

¹/₄ cup lightly roasted pecans, chopped

1 bunch scallions, white part only, finely
    sliced

20 pearl onions, peeled

1¹/₂ cups water

4 tablespoons sweet butter

4 tablespoons sugar

GARNISH

2 chives, chopped

4 chives, greens only

1. Preheat the oven to 375 degrees F.

2. Clean the insides of the pheasants. Remove the pheasant wings and necks and chop. Truss the pheasants. Rub lightly with 2 tablespoons olive oil and season with salt and pepper.

3. Heat 2 tablespoons of olive oil in a roasting pan. When hot, place the pheasants on their sides in the pan and sear over medium to high heat for 3 to 5 minutes. Remove the excess fat and turn the pheasants breast side up. Add the chopped wings and neck, sliced onion, and garlic. Roast in the oven for 30 minutes, occasionally stirring the vegetables and bones to prevent sticking. Remove the pheasants to a platter and discard the necks and wings. Deglaze the roasting pan with 3 cups of chicken stock on top of the stove.

4. Transfer the stock to a 2-quart saucepan and reduce to 1 cup. Add all but 1 tablespoon of cream to the saucepan and simmer gently over low heat for approximately 3 to 5 minutes. In a small bowl, mix the remaining 1 tablespoon cream with the cornstarch to form a smooth paste. Add the mixture to the saucepan and stir until it boils. Simmer for 8 to 10 minutes, occasionally skimming the scum from the top. Strain the sauce through a fine strainer lined with cheesecloth or a *chinois* into another saucepan.

5. Cook the wild rice: Add the rice to 1$^1/_2$ cups of boiling salted water and boil, uncovered, for 5 minutes. Drain and return to the saucepan. Add the remaining chicken stock and season with kosher salt and freshly ground black pepper. Cook covered until all the liquid is absorbed, approximately 25 minutes. Drain.

6. In another saucepan, heat the remaining olive oil and sauté the mushrooms. Add the cooked wild rice, pecans, and scallions. Simmer for 2 to 3 minutes, season with salt and pepper to taste, and add the strained sauce. Keep warm.

7. Meanwhile, in a large skillet combine the pearl onions, water, butter, and sugar over high heat and cook until the water has evaporated and the butter and sugar begin to caramelize the onions, approximately 3 to 5 minutes. Lower the heat and continue to cook until the onions are evenly caramelized. Remove the onions with a slotted spoon to a towel to soak up excess butter.

8. Carve the pheasants by removing the leg and thigh sections. Separate the legs from the thighs and remove the thigh bones. Remove the breasts from the bones; you will have 4 boneless breasts.

9. To serve, spoon the wild rice sauce onto the middle of each dinner plate. Place a breast and a thigh on top of the rice. Arrange caramelized onions around the rice. Sprinkle chopped chives around the plate and top the pheasant with a chive placed on the diagonal.

SERVES 4

This pan-roasted quail has a luscious fruity Port sauce that perfectly complements the game. The '21' Club serves baby carrots, turnips, beets, and tomatoes that add a splash of color to a dish with one of the creamiest herb polentas I have ever tasted.

The legendary '21' Club was a speakeasy during Prohibition and has maintained its celebrity status ever since. Many presidents, including John F. Kennedy and Richard Nixon, have graced its most favored tables.

PAN-ROASTED QUAIL WITH PORT AND HERB POLENTA

THE '21' CLUB

FOR THE QUAIL AND MARINADE

8 fresh semi-boneless quail, breastbones and backbones removed
1/2 cup good dry red wine
1/2 cup good-quality Port, not too sweet
1/4 cup plus 1 tablespoon olive oil
2 tablespoons balsamic vinegar
2 tablespoons dark molasses
2 bay leaves
1 teaspoon cracked black peppercorns
2 garlic cloves, peeled and crushed
several sprigs fresh thyme
1 teaspoon juniper berries, crushed
1 tablespoon sweet butter

PORT SAUCE

2 tablespoons sweet butter
1 shallot, peeled and minced
1/2 teaspoon sugar
1 cup good Port plus 2 tablespoons reserved
1 teaspoon balsamic vinegar
1 cup Game Stock (page 205)
salt and freshly ground pepper to taste

GARNISH

1 orange
4 sprigs parsley

1. If semi-boneless quail is unavailable, split the whole quail down the back through the backbone. Working from the inside, split the bird and free the breastbone from the meat.

2. Make the marinade: Combine the wine, Port, 1/4 cup olive oil, balsamic vinegar, molasses, bay leaves, black peppercorns, garlic, thyme, and juniper berries in a large bowl. Add the quail and marinate overnight to tenderize.

3. Preheat the oven to 450 degrees F.

4. Remove the quail from the marinade. Heat the 1 tablespoon butter and 1 tablespoon olive oil in an ovenproof saucepan over low heat and brown the quail on both sides. Remove the pan from the stove and place it in the oven for 5 minutes.

5. Make the sauce: Remove the excess oil and the quail from the saucepan to a plate. Add 1 tablespoon butter to the pan and sauté the shallot over medium heat. Add the sugar, Port, and balsamic vinegar. Add the game stock and reduce by two-thirds, maintaining a low simmer. Add additional Port to taste, whisk in 1 tablespoon of butter to finish the sauce, and season to taste with salt and pepper.

6. Make the garnish: Remove the zest, skin, seeds, and membranes from the orange. Cut the orange into sections.

7. To serve, arrange the quail and 3 triangles of herb polenta (recipe follows) on each plate and generously pour the Port sauce around the plate. Garnish with orange zest, orange sections, and parsley sprigs.

SERVES 4

HERB POLENTA

T H E   ' 2 1 '   C L U B

1–1¹/₂ quarts milk (or you may
   substitute water)

¹/₂ teaspoon sea salt

1¹/₂ cups yellow cornmeal

1 cup water, as needed

6 tablespoons sweet butter

¹/₄ cup chopped fresh herbs, such as a
   combination of thyme, oregano,
   parsley, or chives

6 tablespoons grated Parmesan cheese

1. In a medium saucepan, combine the milk and the salt and bring almost to a boil. Add the cornmeal in a steady stream, using a whisk to remove the lumps. Simmer the polenta over low heat for 25 minutes, stirring occasionally with a wooden spoon. If it thickens too quickly, add up to 1 cup of water. After 25 minutes, remove the polenta from the heat and add all remaining ingredients, except the Parmesan, stirring them in quickly while the polenta is hot. Pour the polenta onto an 18- × 12-inch baking pan and smooth out evenly to a ¹/₄-inch thickness with the back of a wooden spoon. Let cool at room temperature for 25 to 30 minutes, until firm.

2. Cut the polenta into 2-inch squares, then slice the squares diagonally. Sprinkle the triangles with Parmesan cheese and toast them under the broiler until golden.

S E R V E S   4

VEAL CHOP WITH SAGE AND WHITE WINE AND ROSEMARY POTATOES

IL MULINO

The Masci brothers, some of New York's finest Italian sauciers, recommend only the most succulent first-cut plume of veal in their version of the classic Italian veal chop with sage and shallot-flavored sauce. Il Mulino is named after the windmill in their hometown in the Abruzzi region.

4 veal chops, 14 ounces each

salt and freshly ground pepper

6 tablespoons lightly salted butter

¹/₂ cup plus 2 tablespoons olive oil

4 shallots, peeled and minced

2 tablespoons fresh sage leaves

1 cup dry white wine

8 red potatoes, unpeeled and diced

2 tablespoons fresh rosemary leaves

1. Pound the veal chops lightly and season with salt and pepper.

2. In a large sauté pan, heat 4 tablespoons of butter and 4 tablespoons of the olive oil until hot. Add the veal chops, pressing down on them with a spatula as they cook, turning once. Cook a total of 8 to 10 minutes. Remove the chops and place them on a warm platter. Drain the excess oil from the pan.

3. In the same pan, heat 2 tablespoons of the olive oil and sauté the shallots and sage leaves. When the sage leaves are crispy, remove half of the oil, add the white wine, and reduce over low heat until the sauce thickens.

4. Heat the remaining 4 tablespoons of olive oil in a sauté pan, add the potatoes, and cook halfway. Add the remaining 2 tablespoons of butter and the rosemary and continue to cook until tender.

5. Pour the sauce over the veal chops and serve with the potatoes.

SERVES 4

SLICED FILET OF
VEAL HUNAN STYLE

SHUN LEE

2 eggs

4 tablespoons cornstarch

2 teaspoons vegetable oil

1 pound filet of veal, pounded, cut into
  strips $^1/_2$ inch thick by 1 inch long

SAUCE

2 tablespoons sugar

2 tablespoons sherry

2 tablespoons soy sauce

2 teaspoons white vinegar

2 tablespoons Light Chicken Stock (page
  203)

1 teaspoon cornstarch dissolved in 2
  teaspoons water

2 teaspoons sesame oil

$^1/_2$ cup vegetable oil

$^2/_3$ cup red bell peppers, seeded and cut
  into 1-inch squares

2 cups fresh straw mushrooms

12 fresh water chestnuts, peeled and
  sliced

$^1/_2$ pound snow pea pods

2 scallions, peeled and minced

2 garlic cloves, peeled and finely chopped

$^1/_2$ teaspoon peeled minced ginger

2 tablespoons chili paste (or 2 red hot
  cherry peppers ground in 6 teaspoons
  vegetable oil)

This tender sliced filet of veal,
adorned with fresh straw
mushrooms, sits in a tantalizingly
piquant sauce comprised of hot chili
paste, scallions, garlic, and sherry.
Red peppers, straw mushrooms,
and crisp snow peas garnish this
Hunan specialty.

1. In a small bowl, mix together the eggs, cornstarch, and 2 teaspoons of
vegetable oil. Add the veal and marinate for 15 minutes. Remove the veal
from the marinade with a slotted spoon.

2. Make the sauce: Mix together the sugar and sherry and add the soy sauce.
Stir in the white vinegar. Add the chicken stock and the cornstarch mixture
and stir together. Add the sesame oil and combine. Reserve.

3. Heat the vegetable oil in a wok until very hot. Add the veal, bell peppers,
straw mushrooms, and water chestnuts and stir-fry until the veal browns and
is three-quarters cooked, approximately 3 minutes. Strain the entire mixture
through a sieve to remove the excess oil.

4. Add the pea pods, scallions, garlic, ginger, and chili paste and stir-fry. Then
add the veal mixture and stir-fry for another minute. Add the sauce and stir-
fry rapidly to heat through. Serve with steamed rice.

SERVES 4

117

*These sautéed venison medallions
are intensely flavored and
extraordinarily well balanced.
Caramelized lingonberries provide
a dynamic contrast to the sauce of
crushed peppercorns, sweet
Sauternes, and orange juice. Game
is one of the specialties at Le
Régence, a favorite for Christmas
and New Year's celebrations, and it
is no wonder that the restaurant
has received four stars from* Forbes
*and is considered one of the top ten
New York restaurants.*

VENISON MEDALLIONS WITH PEPPERCORN SAUCE, CHESTNUTS, APPLES, RED CABBAGE, AND LINGONBERRIES

LE REGENCE

SAUCE

3 shallots, peeled and sliced

2 tablespoons sweet butter

2 tablespoons crushed black peppercorns

$^1/_2$ cup red wine vinegar

2 tablespoons berry jelly (preferably raspberry)

3 cups venison stock (substitute venison bones for veal bones in Brown Veal Stock, page 207)

salt and freshly ground white pepper to taste

LINGONBERRY JAM

1 cup freshly squeezed orange juice

1 cup Sauternes wine

6 ounces fresh lingonberries

1 bunch fresh basil, stemmed and julienned

1 bunch mint, stemmed and chopped

1 orange, unpeeled, cut into segments

3 Granny Smith apples

2 tablespoons water, if needed

1 tablespoon sweet butter

18 chestnuts, blanched, peeled, and halved

salt and pepper to taste

6 tablespoons Clarified Butter (page 196)

$^3/_4$ pound wild mushrooms, cleaned and sliced (shiitake, pied de mouton)

$^1/_3$ cup seedless red grapes, halved

1 pound red cabbage, julienned

2 tablespoons julienned ginger

6 nests of angel hair or cappellini pasta

2 tablespoons chopped fresh herbs, such as basil, sage, tarragon, or rosemary

$2^1/_2$ pounds saddle of venison (12 medallions, 3 ounces each)

GARNISH

1 bunch chervil

1. Make the sauce: In a large saucepan, sauté the shallots in 1 tablespoon of butter and add the crushed peppercorns. Add the red wine vinegar and reduce by three-quarters. Add the berry jelly and cook until lightly caramelized. Pour in the venison stock and reduce slowly by half until it coats the back of a spoon, approximately 45 minutes. Then whisk in 1 tablespoon butter and salt and pepper to taste. Reheat when ready to serve.

2. Make the jam: In a saucepan, bring the orange juice, Sauternes, lingonberries, basil, mint, and orange segments to a boil. After 3 to 5 minutes of boiling, remove the lingonberries and reserve. Reduce the liquid until it becomes syrupy, about 30 minutes. Return the lingonberries to the pan and bring to a boil again. Let the jam cool.

3. Peel and core the apples and cut each apple into 6 slices (the skin can be left on, if desired, for a more attractive presentation). In a saucepan, melt 1 tablespoon of butter and sauté the apples and the chestnuts until the apples soften, approximately 5 to 6 minutes. Add 2 tablespoons of water if moisture is required to soften the apples. Season with salt and pepper to taste and keep warm.

4. In a saucepan, melt 1 tablespoon of the clarified butter and sauté the wild mushrooms, red grapes, red cabbage, and 1 teaspoon of the ginger over high heat for approximately 2 minutes. Add salt and pepper to taste and keep warm.

5. In another pan, sauté the remaining ginger in 1 tablespoon of hot clarified butter until crispy. Drain the ginger on paper towels to remove the excess butter.

6. Cook the pasta: Bring a large pot of salted water to a rapid boil. Add the angel hair pasta and cook for 3 minutes, or until *al dente*. Drain the pasta and toss well with the chopped herbs. Keep warm.

7. Season the venison medallions with salt and pepper. In a large sauté pan, melt 4 tablespoons of clarified butter and sauté the venison on both sides over high heat until browned, approximately 3 minutes. Sauté them over medium heat for approximately 2 minutes or until cooked as desired.

8. To serve, place a mound of the red cabbage mixture in the center of each plate, top with 2 venison medallions side by side, and alternate 3 apple slices and 3 chestnuts around the cabbage mixture. Place the jam alongside the venison. Pour the sauce over the meat and top with sautéed ginger. Garnish with chervil. Serve the pasta on the side of the plate or in a separate bowl.

SERVES 6

FISH AND SHELLFISH

Although once considered a poor man's fish, "cod is doing swimmingly," according to New York Times *food writer Dena Kleiman. Many of New York's great restaurants have recognized its culinary merit and are serving it to increased demand. Olives and tomatoes, indigenous to Provence, add a piquancy that heightens the flavor.*

Classically trained in French culinary techniques, Chef Charles Palmer drew his inspiration for this dish from Mougins, France. His formidable talent makes him one of America's top chefs.

PAN-ROASTED COD WITH SWEET GARLIC PAN AU JUS AND NICOISE OIL

AUREOLE

SWEET GARLIC SAUCE

1 head garlic, separated into unpeeled
  cloves
1 teaspoon plus 2 tablespoons olive oil
2 tablespoons Clarified Butter (page
  196)
1 cup mirepoix (chopped carrot, onion,
  and celery)
1¼ cups strong Fish Stock (page 204)
1 small herb bouquet tied in cheesecloth:
  1 tablespoon chopped parsley
  2 sprigs thyme
  1 bay leaf
  18 peppercorns

NICOISE OIL

¼ cup niçoise olives, pitted and chopped
1 tablespoon fines herbes: *fresh chopped
  parsley, chervil, tarragon, and chives*
2 tablespoons sweet butter
2 tablespoons olive oil

COD

four 6-ounce cod filets, fat removed
salt and freshly ground white pepper to
  taste
4 tablespoons olive oil or safflower oil
2 tablespoons sweet butter

2 medium fennel bulbs
2 tablespoons Clarified Butter
  (page 196)

GARNISH

1 tomato, blanched, skinned, seeded, and
  cut into ¼-inch cubes
4 sprigs chervil

1. Make the sweet garlic sauce: Preheat the oven to 350 degrees F. Toss the unpeeled garlic cloves with 1 teaspoon olive oil and roast in a baking pan for 20 minutes. Remove the skins from the cloves.

2. In a medium saucepan, heat 2 tablespoons clarified butter and sweat the *mirepoix* with 6 peeled garlic cloves until soft. Reserve the remaining cloves for garnish. Add the fish stock and herb bouquet and reduce by half. Strain the sauce and set aside.

3. Make the niçoise oil: Mix the olives, *fines herbes*, butter, and olive oil in a blender until smooth.

4. Season the cod filets with salt and pepper. In a nonstick pan, heat the oil until very hot and sear the filets until browned on both sides. Add the butter. (If the filets are very thick, transfer to a preheated 450 degree F. oven and cook for 2 to 3 minutes.) Remove from pan and keep warm.

5. Discard the excess oil from the pan and return the pan to the top of the stove. Add the reserved sauce and bring it to a boil over medium heat. Reduce the sauce until slightly thickened, or until it evenly coats the back of a spoon, approximately 5 minutes. Adjust the seasoning to taste.

6. Peel and cut the fennel bulbs into 2- $\times$ $1/4$-inch long sticks. Blanch in salted boiling water. Drain. Melt the clarified butter in a sauté pan and heat the fennel batons.

7. To serve, place fennel batons in the center of each plate and top with a fish filet. Cover the filets with the sweet garlic sauce and niçoise olive oil. Place the diced tomato around the plate inside the rim. Garnish with a chervil sprig and a few roasted garlic cloves.

SERVES 4

Inside the lightly breaded exterior of these crab cakes are flaky morsels of crabmeat mixed with crunchy celery dice. Served in a pool of grainy Pommery mustard sauce, these cakes are adorned with fried lotus slivers, a garnish originated by the Chinese generations ago.

The Four Seasons, the interior of which has been designated a historic landmark, was designed by the renowned architect Philip Johnson. Lots of deals are made during lunchtime and dinner, particularly in The Grill Room, the favored room of Michael Korda, Don Madden, Felix Rohatyan, and Bill Blass, among other prominent citizens.

CRAB CAKES WITH FRIED LOTUS ROOT

THE FOUR SEASONS

1 cup vegetable oil

$^1/_2$ lotus root, peeled and finely sliced

1 dill pickle, chopped medium fine

1 stalk celery, minced

1 pound fresh lump crabmeat, shells and cartilage removed

1 egg yolk

$^3/_4$ cup mayonnaise

6 slices dry white bread, crusts removed

2 tablespoons sweet butter

2 tablespoons Light Chicken Stock (page 203)

2 tablespoons milk

4 tablespoons Pommery mustard

$^1/_4$ teaspoon salt

$^1/_8$ teaspoon freshly ground pepper

1 tablespoon mustard seed, crushed

1 teaspoon ground turmeric

1 teaspoon curry powder

$^1/_2$ teaspoon paprika

SAUCE

2 tablespoons sweet butter

2 tablespoons flour

1. In a deep saucepan, heat the vegetable oil until piping hot, to approximately 350 degrees F. Fry the lotus root until golden, approximately $1^1/_2$ minutes. Place on a paper towel to drain.

2. Mix the pickle, celery, crabmeat, egg yolk, and mayonnaise together. Firmly press the mixture into eight 2- × 3-inch oval patties.

3. Place the bread in a blender and process until finely ground. Coat the crab cakes well with the crumbs, pouring them over the cakes until the cakes are no longer sticky.

4. Melt the butter in a saucepan over very low heat and slowly cook the crab cakes until golden brown on both sides. Keep warm.

5. Make the sauce: In a saucepan, melt the butter and add the flour, stirring with a wooden spoon. Add the chicken stock and milk and cook for 10 minutes. Add the Pommery mustard, salt, pepper, mustard seed, turmeric, curry powder, and paprika and cook for 10 minutes.

6. Serve 2 crab cakes per person, drizzle with sauce, and garnish with the fried lotus root.

HINTS FROM THE CHEF: It is better to cook the crab cakes in a nonstick pan. Do not overpower the sauce with curry. The taste should be very subtle. Instead of lotus root, parsnips, parsley, spinach, or yams can be used for the fried garnish.

SERVES 4

*Southwestern cuisine derives
primarily from the culinary
traditions of Spain and Mexico.
This fanciful grilled halibut, served
with a zesty lime yogurt cream and
dotted with red and yellow pepper
pesto, includes pungently seasoned
okra. The combination is truly
sublime.*

GRILLED HALIBUT WITH MARINATED SUMMER TOMATOES

ARIZONA 206

CORNMEAL SEASONING
1 cup cornmeal
1 teaspoon ground cumin
1 teaspoon ancho chili powder
1 teaspoon salt
$^1/_4$ teaspoon cayenne pepper

MARINATED TOMATOES
$^1/_2$ cup balsamic vinegar
$^1/_4$ cup olive oil
2 tablespoons basil chiffonnade (cut
    into thin strips)
salt and freshly ground black pepper to
    taste
6 beefsteak tomatoes, chopped

ROASTED PEPPER PESTO
1 cup watercress, stems removed
1 cup basil leaves, stems removed
$^1/_4$ cup capers
splash of olive oil

salt to taste
1 roasted red bell pepper, peeled, seeded,
    and chopped
1 roasted yellow bell pepper, peeled,
    seeded, and chopped

LIME YOGURT CREAM
$^1/_2$ cup plain yogurt
$^1/_2$ cup sour cream
grated zest and juice of 2 limes
dash of Tabasco
salt to taste

$1^1/_2$ cups sliced okra, cut on the diagonal
3 tablespoons sweet butter

six 6-ounce halibut filets

GARNISH
18 radishes, leaves attached
6 basil leaves

1. Make the cornmeal seasoning: In a small bowl, mix together the cornmeal, cumin, ancho chili powder, salt, and cayenne.

2. Marinate the tomatoes: Mix together the balsamic vinegar, olive oil, basil, salt and freshly ground pepper to taste in a bowl. Add the chopped tomatoes and marinate for $^1/_2$ hour.

3. Make the roasted pepper pesto: In a food processor, combine the watercress, basil leaves, capers, olive oil, and salt to taste. Process well, add the roasted red and yellow peppers, and process again until the mixture is smooth.

4. Make the lime yogurt cream: In a bowl, mix together the yogurt, sour cream, zest and juice of the limes, Tabasco, and salt.

5. Dredge the sliced okra in the seasoned cornmeal. Place the okra in a strainer and shake to remove the excess cornmeal. In a saucepan, heat the 3 tablespoons butter and sauté the okra until very crispy.

6. Grill the halibut either on a stove-top grill or in the broiler until tender.

7. To serve, place the halibut in the center of the plate. Arrange marinated tomatoes on one side; sprinkle crispy okra over them. Surround the tomatoes with 3 radishes. Drizzle the lime yogurt cream over the tomatoes and okra sparingly. Garnish each halibut filet with a dollop of pesto and a basil leaf.

N O T E :   The yogurt cream and pesto may be made 6 to 12 hours in advance and should be kept covered in the refrigerator. Ancho chiles are pear shaped, semi-hot, dried red chiles. The fresh variety is called poblano.

S E R V E S 6

An internationally recognized culinary giant, Seppi Renggli reigned over The Four Seasons for many years. He originated its renowned spa cuisine and was one of the first chefs to offer seasonal menus.

This luscious steamed seafood with fragrant vegetables demonstrates his gravitation toward healthier foods high in nutrients and low in fat and sodium.

The key to steaming, one of the oldest methods of cooking, is to never allow the food to touch the water. The Oriental bamboo basket, used here, produces the best results.

SEAFOOD STEAMED IN BAMBOO WITH SAVOY CABBAGE, BROCCOLI RABE, AND LEMONGRASS

THE SEA GRILL

4 leaves of Savoy cabbage

four 6- to 8-ounce fleshy fish filets, such
    as salmon filets, or skinless tuna
    steaks, sea scallops, or black bass filets

4 scallions, halved lengthwise

8 baby carrots, peeled and sliced
    lengthwise

8 asparagus, $^1/_4$ of the stalk ends cut off

1 bunch broccoli rabe *or* baby bok
    choy

4 small white onions, peeled and halved

4 large shiitake mushrooms, stems
    removed

1 small seedless cucumber, cut into
    quarters lengthwise

1 tablespoon coarse sea salt

$^1/_2$ teaspoon cracked black pepper

3 garlic cloves, peeled

2 to 3 lime leaves or $^1/_2$ stalk of
    lemongrass, split (if not available, use
    lime or lemon zest)

HERB OIL

$^1/_2$ cup olive oil

$^1/_2$ cup chopped herbs (chives, Italian
    parsley, chervil, tarragon)

2 teaspoons cracked black pepper

juice of 2 lemons

GARNISH

black and red cracked peppercorns

1. Half fill a large sauté pan—which will hold the bamboo steamer—with water and bring it to a boil. Line a 9- to 12-inch bamboo steamer with 4 leaves of cabbage. Arrange the fish pieces on top of the cabbage. Then arrange all the vegetables in evenly distributed positions on top like a flower arrangement. All the vegetables should be arranged to achieve a beautiful array of colors.

2. Sprinkle the vegetables and fish with salt, pepper, garlic cloves. Artfully place lemongrass blades on top. Steam, covered, for 4 to 5 minutes. Turn the heat off and let rest for 3 to 4 minutes.

3. Make the herb oil: Combine all the ingredients and let the herbs infuse in the oil in an airtight jar.

4. To serve, arrange the fish and vegetables on dinner plates. Alternatively, serve in the bamboo steamer, placed on a large plate. Serve with the herb oil either in separate bowls or on the fish. Garnish with the cracked peppercorns.

SERVES 4

*French lentils dotted with bacon,
marjoram, and thyme add crunchy
texture and aromatic flavor to this
hearty salmon creation. The red
wine sauce gives the salmon robust
flavoring, which accompanied by a
Chassagne Montrachet from one of
France's premier wine-producing
regions affords a gustatory delight.*

SALMON WITH LENTILS AND RED WINE SAUCE

MONTRACHET

1/2 cup French green lentils	RED WINE SAUCE
1 quart water	*1 tablespoon sweet butter*
2 tablespoons olive oil	*1/2 pound salmon bones or other fish*
1 tablespoon finely minced garlic	*bones, cut into small pieces*
1 tablespoon finely chopped shallots	*1 teaspoon finely minced garlic*
4 strips of bacon, finely chopped into	*1/3 cup shallots, peeled and coarsely*
cubes	*chopped*
2 teaspoons chopped fresh thyme	*1/3 cup chopped leek greens*
1 tablespoon chopped fresh marjoram	*1/2 cup chopped celery*
salt and freshly ground white pepper to	*2 sprigs fresh thyme*
taste	*1 cup Light Chicken Stock (page 203)*
1 cup heavy cream	*1 1/2 cups red Rhône wine*
	salt and pepper to taste

*eight 1 1/2-ounce salmon filets, boneless,
skinless, and thinly sliced 1/4 inch
thick*

1. In a large saucepan, soak the lentils overnight in 1 quart of water. Salt the water and bring to a boil. Stir and simmer for 10 minutes, until the lentils are cooked *al dente*. Drain.

2. Heat the olive oil in a casserole, stir in the garlic, shallots, and bacon, and cook for 2 to 3 minutes, but do not brown. Add the drained lentils, thyme, marjoram, salt and pepper, and simmer for 8 minutes. Add the heavy cream, bring to a boil, and let simmer for a few minutes.

3. Make the red wine sauce: Melt 1 tablespoon of the butter in a large saucepan. Add the fish bones, garlic, shallots, leeks, celery, and thyme. Cook over medium heat, stirring, for about 5 minutes. Add the chicken stock, red wine, and salt and pepper, and bring to a boil. Simmer for 20 minutes.

4. Strain and push the sauce through a fine sieve into a saucepan. Simmer until reduced to about 1/2 cup, approximately 15 minutes, and adjust the seasoning.

5. Place ¹/₂ cup or more of the lentil mixture in the center of each of 4 ovenproof plates. Cover the lentils with 2 slices of salmon, then season with salt and pepper.

6. Place the broiler rack about 4 inches from the heat source. Place each plate on the rack and broil for about 1 minute, or until the salmon is done.

7. To serve, spoon about 3 tablespoons of the red wine sauce around the salmon on each plate. Serve with fresh steamed snow peas or snap peas and asparagus tips.

SERVES 4

Aquavit, or "water of life," the potent potato-distilled vodka for which the restaurant is named, is the perfect prelude to this one-sided sautéed salmon. Although for many smorgasbord and herring come to mind, Scandinavian cuisine actually mirrors classic French cooking. This chive butter sauce, accompanied by earthy mushrooms, is a contemporary derivative of the French beurre blanc.

Simple presentations and refined sauces as demonstrated here distinguish Aquavit, which is celebrated not only for its fresh fish, but also for its flavorful game dishes.

ONE-SIDED SAUTEED SALMON WITH CHIVE BUTTER SAUCE AND WILD MUSHROOMS

AQUAVIT

¹/₂ pound plus 2 tablespoons sweet butter, cut into 4 or more pieces, softened
³/₄ cup finely chopped chives
¹/₂ cup finely chopped parsley
1 tablespoon fresh lemon juice
¹/₄ cup Fish Stock (page 204) or clam juice
¹/₂ cup dry white wine
coarse salt and freshly ground white pepper to taste

2 cups mixed wild mushrooms, left whole if small; sliced in half if large
6 fresh Norwegian salmon filets, 8 ounces each, scales removed but skin left on
3 tablespoons olive oil

GARNISH
¹/₄ cup chives cut into 2-inch sticks

1. Make the herb butter: In a food processor, blend ¹/₂ pound butter, chives, and parsley for 3 minutes. Add the lemon juice and process again quickly. When the mixture is smooth and a bright green, strain through a fine sieve, using a spatula to push it through.

2. In a large saucepan over medium heat, combine the fish stock and white wine and reduce by three-quarters, until almost evaporated. Slowly whisk in the herb-butter mixture, and season with salt and white pepper to taste. Place the sauce in a stainless steel bowl (to prevent it from separating) and cover with plastic wrap. Keep warm.

3. Melt the remaining 2 tablespoons of butter in a sauté pan and sauté the mushrooms until firm but not wilted.

4. Season the skinless side of the salmon with coarse salt and white pepper. Heat the olive oil in a large nonstick skillet, and sauté the salmon over low heat, skin side down, for approximately 10 to 15 minutes, depending on the thickness. (A 1-inch-thick piece of salmon will be rare after 10 minutes.) Do not turn.

5. To serve, generously spoon sauce onto warm plates and place a salmon filet in the center. Garnish artfully with the mushrooms and remaining chives, cut into 2-inch sticks.

SERVES 6

SHRIMP SZECHUAN

SHUN LEE

HOT RED PEPPER PASTE
2 dried red hot chili peppers
6 tablespoons olive oil

SAUCE
4 tablespoons sugar
6 tablespoons tomato ketchup
1 tablespoon soy sauce
6 tablespoons sherry (or if available, 3
  tablespoons rice wine and 3
  tablespoons sherry)
6 tablespoons Light Chicken Stock (page
  203)

1 cup plus 4 tablespoons vegetable oil
20 jumbo shrimp, shelled and deveined
1 tablespoon chopped garlic
2 tablespoons chopped ginger
6 tablespoons chopped scallions, greens
  only
2 tablespoons chopped red bell pepper
4 tablespoons finely chopped bamboo
  shoots
1 tablespoon cornstarch dissolved in 3
  tablespoons water
drop of sesame oil

This shrimp dish originated in the southwestern Chinese province of Szechuan, where the food is generally spicy. The combination of ginger, garlic, scallions, and marinated hot peppers creates the fire in this transcendent Chinese creation.

1. Make the hot red pepper paste: Grind the hot red peppers in oil with a mortar and pestle to create a paste. Let stand for 1 hour.

2. Make the sauce: In a bowl, combine the sugar and ketchup. Add the soy sauce, sherry, and chicken stock.

3. Heat 1 cup of vegetable oil in a wok until very hot. Add the shrimp and stir-fry for 1 minute. Remove the shrimp and discard the excess oil.

4. Add 4 tablespoons of vegetable oil to the wok and when smoking, add the garlic, ginger, scallions, red bell pepper, 1 tablespoon of the hot red pepper paste, and the bamboo shoots. Stir-fry for 30 seconds, then stir in the sauce.

5. Return the shrimp to the wok, add the cornstarch mixture and a drop of sesame oil, and stir-fry continuously so that the food does not stick. Serve immediately with steamed white rice.

NOTE: Hot red pepper paste is available at Oriental markets.

SERVES 4

*These perfectly seared scallops
accented with earthy shiitake
mushrooms are artfully presented
with a confetti of colors: The vivid
red, yellow, and green bell peppers
are evocative of the colors used by
Italian Renaissance artist Giacomo
Bellini. The frothy combination of
white peach nectar and champagne,
also called a Bellini, originated
with Harry Cipriani's father,
Giuseppe, in Venice in the thirties.
In fact, this same sublime
concoction inspired Cipriani's latest
novel,* Heloise and Bellinis.

BAY SCALLOPS BELLINI

HARRY CIPRIANI

1/4 pound shiitake *mushrooms*

6 tablespoons sweet butter, softened

2 stalks celery, chopped medium

1 medium onion, peeled and chopped

*2 leeks, white part only, thoroughly
washed and chopped*

*1 cup plus 2 tablespoons dry white
vermouth or dry sherry*

2 cups heavy cream

*salt and freshly ground white pepper to
taste*

*2 tablespoons cold sweet butter, cut into
bits*

1/2 cup seeded, diced red bell pepper

1/2 cup seeded, diced yellow bell pepper

1/2 cup seeded, diced green bell pepper

2 pounds bay scallops, rinsed and dried

all-purpose flour for dusting

2 tablespoons olive oil

GARNISH

*1/2 bunch Italian parsley, stemmed and
chopped*

1. Rinse the *shiitake* mushrooms by placing them in a strainer and dipping
quickly in bottled water. Remove the mushrooms from the strainer and slice
thin.

2. In a large saucepan, heat 4 tablespoons of the butter over medium heat.
Add the celery, onion, leeks, and mushrooms and cook, stirring occasionally,
until the vegetables are softened and translucent, approximately 15 minutes.

3. In the same pan, off the stove, add 1 cup of the vermouth and return to
the stove to reduce. Cook over high heat and reduce for approximately 3
minutes. Lower the heat to medium and whisk in the cream. Boil until
reduced by half, approximately 10 minutes. Strain the sauce through a *chinois*,
pressing hard on the vegetables to release the juices, return the sauce to the
pan, and cook over low heat for a few minutes to thicken. Season with salt
and pepper. Off the stove, whisk in the cold butter bits until incorporated.
Reserve.

4. Melt the remaining 2 tablespoons of butter in a large skillet over medium
heat and add the diced peppers, stirring occasionally, until slightly softened.
Remove from the pan and reserve.

5. Season the scallops with salt and white pepper, dust them lightly with
flour, and shake them in a sieve to remove the excess flour.

6. Heat the oil in a medium saucepan over high heat, add the scallops, and
brown on both sides, approximately 3 minutes. Discard the excess oil. Off the
stove, add the remaining 2 tablespoons of vermouth and return to the stove to

flambé, cooking for 1 minute. Add the reserved cream sauce and bring to a boil.

7. To serve, place the scallops on plates, and spoon sauce around and on top of the scallops. Sprinkle with the diced pepper. Garnish with chopped Italian parsley. Serve with short-grain rice such as Arborio.

SERVES 6

*White beans are typical hearty fare
in southwestern France. The rich,
syrupy, old wine vinegar and Port
sauce provides a lovely contrast to
the starkness of the white skate
flesh. This tasty yet inexpensive
fish has gained popularity in New
York's fine eating establishments,
like Park Bistro, where lace
curtains, Mason jars of vegetables,
and photographs of Simone
Signoret and Jean Cocteau set the
scene.*

SAUTEED SKATE, OLD WINE VINEGAR SAUCE, AND WHITE BEANS

PARK BISTRO

*4 cups white coco (French navy) beans or
   other dried white imported beans*

1 quart water

1 tablespoon kosher or rock salt

1 carrot, peeled

1/2 medium Spanish onion, peeled

1 bay leaf

1 stem fresh thyme

SAUCE

2 cups balsamic vinegar

2 cups Port

2 cups Light Chicken Stock (page 203)

salt and freshly ground pepper to taste

2 tablespoons sweet butter

2 tablespoons sweet butter

1 tablespoon water

1 tablespoon chopped shallot

*salt and freshly ground white pepper to
   taste*

1 bunch Italian parsley, chopped

2 skates, skinned and fileted

*2 tablespoons Clarified Butter
   (page 196)*

GARNISH

4 stems Italian parsley or chervil

coarsely ground black pepper to taste

1. Soften the beans by soaking them in 1 quart of water in the refrigerator overnight. Drain.

2. Cook the beans in 2 quarts of water. After the beans have been cooking for 10 minutes, add the salt, carrot, onion, bay leaf, and thyme and continue cooking an additional 10 minutes until tender. Rinse under cold water and strain.

3. Make the sauce: In a large saucepan over medium heat, heat and reduce the balsamic vinegar until almost dry, making sure not to burn the mixture. Add the Port and reduce by half. Add the chicken stock and reduce by half again. Season with salt and pepper. Slowly whisk in 2 tablespoons of butter over low heat. Keep warm.

4. In a large saucepan, heat 2 tablespoons of butter with 1 tablespoon water. Add the bean mixture and the shallot, and cook over low heat until the shallot is translucent. Season well with salt and pepper. Just before the beans are completely cooked, add the chopped parsley.

5. Season both sides of the skate with salt and white pepper. Heat the clarified butter in a very hot pan and cook the fish until the skate is beautifully browned on one side. Drain on a cloth towel.

6. To serve, place both halves of the skate together so that they look like one piece. Spoon beans on the arch of the skate and spoon the sauce around the platter. Garnish the beans with a stem of parsley or chervil. Add freshly cracked black pepper to the skate sauce.

HINT FROM THE CHEF: Since skate is a cartilaginous fish, it is difficult to remove the skin and bones. Thus it is advisable to ask the fish market to prepare the skate.

SERVES 4

SHELLFISH PAELLA

SOLERA

1 cup extra-virgin olive oil plus 2
    tablespoons for drizzling

4 tablespoons minced onion

2 tomatoes, skinned, seeded, and finely
    chopped

2 cups short-grain rounded white rice

4 cups Shellfish Stock (page 206),
    brought to a boil

1 teaspoon saffron threads

2 bay leaves

1/2 teaspoon hot or medium sweet
    paprika

24 cultivated mussels

24 Manila clams

2 fresh lobster tails (and optional pincers)

4 tablespoons shelled fresh peas

2 tablespoons pimiento strips

16 large shrimp, shelled and deveined

GARNISH

1/2 cup minced parsley

3 tablespoons minced tarragon

1/2 bunch chives, finely chopped

The rice fields of Valencia, in the
Levante, produce the special rice
that is a key ingredient in paella.
Purists are adamant about the
texture of their rice; it should not
be creamy like risotto, but moist
and firm. This consistency is
achieved by "extension," or cooking
the rice in a wide, low-sided paella
pan on top of the stove. The pan
should never be moved after the
liquid has been added. Evaporation
of the stock in this manner allows
the grains of rice to remain separate
and still absorb the proper amount
of liquid.

    Lobster, shrimp, Manila clams,
and mussels enrich this well-
balanced paella. Both the fruity
extra-virgin olive oil and the fresh
herb garnish enhance the saffron-
scented rice.

1. Heat the olive oil in a large 12- to 14-inch paella pan over two burners.
Add the onion and cook until translucent; then add the tomatoes.

2. Over medium heat, add the rice and stir with a wooden spoon, moving
the pan continuously. Cook until the rice turns a very light nutmeg color.
Add all but a few tablespoons of the boiling stock and bring to a simmer,
smoothing out the rice with a wooden spoon. Crush the saffron threads in
your hands and add to the pan. Then add the bay leaves and paprika.

3. Clean the mussels and the clams. Twist the tails off the lobsters and split
them in half lengthwise with a sharp knife. Place them, shell side down, in
the middle of the rice and add the peas and pimientos. As the rice starts to
show through the stock (approximately 5 minutes after you add the lobsters),
place the mussels decoratively around the edges of the pan. Then add an
inner row of clams, and let simmer a few minutes more. Place the shrimp
around the lobsters. Turn the lobster over and cook for an additional 5
minutes. Press down on the seafood so that it absorbs some of the stock. If
the rice seems too dry, add a few extra tablespoons of boiling stock as needed.
Sample the rice when most of the liquid has evaporated. Turn off the heat
and let the paella stand for 10 to 15 minutes before serving. Check to make
sure that all the shellfish have opened. Discard any that have not. Drizzle 1 to
2 tablespoons of the olive oil over the rice mixture and sprinkle with parsley,
tarragon, and chives. The total cooking time for the paella should be
approximately 20 minutes.

SERVES 4 TO 6

*This sensational sea bass wrapped
in buttery Yucca gold potatoes
adorns a luscious bed of
caramelized leeks surrounded by a
delicate red wine sauce. Based upon
the classic culinary technique of
cooking* en papillote *to seal in the
juices, here the parchment is
replaced by overlapping, thinly
sliced potatoes. This dazzling
presentation is representative of the
culinary masterpieces of Le Cirque
and illustrates why Le Cirque is
the ultimate in elegant indulgence.*

ROASTED SEA BASS WRAPPED IN CRISPY POTATO CRUST WITH RED WINE SAUCE AND BRAISED LEEKS

LE CIRQUE

*two 2-pound sea bass, cleaned, fileted,
    and skin removed*
*salt and freshly ground white pepper to
    taste*
*2 large Yucca gold potatoes (or Idaho
    potatoes), peeled*
*3 tablespoons Clarified Butter, melted
    (page 196)*
*2 leeks, quartered lengthwise and rinsed
    well*

9 tablespoons sweet butter
1 bottle Barolo red wine
3 shallots, peeled and chopped
1 fresh sprig thyme
3 tablespoons heavy cream
1 teaspoon sugar

GARNISH
12 chives, sliced into 1-inch lengths

1. Cut the fish filets into pieces 2¹/₂ inches wide by 6 inches long, shaping
the filet tightly. Season with salt and pepper.

2. Slice the potatoes with a *mandoline* or by hand into very thin lengthwise
slices. Toss the potato slices in 1 tablespoon melted clarified butter, adding a
touch of salt. On a baking pan lined with plastic wrap, line up 3 or 4 potato
slices vertically, overlapping them slightly. Place the fish horizontally over the
potatoes and wrap the fish by folding the potato slices over one another.
Repeat for all the fish pieces. Wrap each portion tightly with plastic wrap
and refrigerate for approximately 1 hour.

3. Season the leeks with salt and pepper to taste. In a saucepan over low heat,
sweat the leeks in 1 tablespoon of the sweet butter until soft, covering the pan
with parchment.

4. In a saucepan, reduce the red wine with the shallots and thyme until the
wine has almost evaporated and just covers the shallots. Over low heat, slowly
add the heavy cream and bring to a boil. Whisk in the remaining 8
tablespoons butter, salt and pepper to taste, and sugar, continuing to cook just
until the butter is incorporated. Strain the sauce through a fine-mesh sieve or
chinois into a clean pan. Keep warm.

5. Remove the plastic wrap from the fish. In a hot nonstick pan heat the remaining 2 tablespoons clarified butter. Sauté the fish packets until golden brown on both sides. If the fish is not sufficiently cooked, finish in a preheated 350 degree F. oven for a few minutes.

6. To serve, place the leeks in the middle of each dinner plate and top with the fish. Spoon sauce around the plate and garnish with the 3 chive sticks.

SERVES 4

The technique of searing produces a crisp skin that seals in and enhances the flavor. This pan-seared bass with a light and colorful red pepper sauce has been popular since Chef Seppi Renggli introduced his spa cuisine at The Four Seasons over twenty years ago. Trout or Arctic char can be satisfactorily substituted for the bass.

PAN-SEARED STRIPED BASS WITH RED PEPPER SAUCE AND PEA PODS

THE SEA GRILL

RED PEPPER SAUCE
2 tablespoons olive oil
1 small onion, chopped
2 garlic cloves, chopped
1/4 teaspoon crushed dried hot red pepper
   flakes or jalapeño pepper, chopped
2 red bell peppers, seeded and cut into
   1-inch dice
2 beefsteak tomatoes, seeded and cut into
   1-inch dice

1/2 pound pea pods or sugar snap peas

four 8-ounce striped bass filets, with skin
2 tablespoons olive oil
2 teaspoons kosher salt

1. Make the red pepper sauce: In a saucepan, heat the olive oil and sauté the onion and garlic for approximately 3 to 4 minutes. Add the hot pepper flakes and simmer for 10 minutes. Let the mixture cool. Pour the mixture into a blender or food processor, add the red pepper and tomato dice, and purée. Press the purée while straining it through a fine-mesh sieve or *chinois* into a saucepan. Bring the sauce to a boil. Gently heat the sauce prior to serving.

2. Blanch the pea pods in salted boiling water for 3 minutes. Drain.

3. While the pea pods are cooking, make incisions in the skin side of the fish, 1/4 inch apart. Arrange the fish, skin side down, in a hot lightly oiled cast-iron skillet and season well with kosher salt. Cook over medium heat for 7 to 9 minutes on the stove on one side only.

4. Serve the fish piping hot surrounded with pea pods and red pepper sauce.

HINT FROM THE CHEF: The key to searing fish is to cook it for only 10 minutes per inch of thickness. Cook the fish only on one side so that it is rare on top. The seared skin should be crisp and tasty.

SERVES 4

Rosa Mexicano, or "Mexican Pink," presents sophisticated authentic Mexican cuisine in a romantic setting. This red snapper topped with salsa cruda, a popular accompaniment to Mexican fare, is assertively flavored with jalapeño peppers. Chef-proprietor Josefina Howard serves this classic dish with "Mexican" rice, flavored with chicken stock and onion.

RED SNAPPER IN SALSA CRUDA

ROSA MEXICANO

THE SALSA

3 medium ripe tomatoes, seeded and diced

1 small bunch coriander, finely chopped, to taste

3 fresh jalapeño peppers, seeds and veins removed, and finely chopped

1 large white onion, peeled and finely chopped

juice of 1 lemon

2 pounds red snapper filets, with skin, cut into 2-inch-wide slices

salt and freshly ground black pepper to taste

RICE

1 Spanish onion, peeled and minced

1 garlic clove, peeled and sliced

3 tablespoons vegetable oil

1 1/2 cups long-grain white rice

3 cups Light Chicken Stock (page 203)

2 tablespoons olive oil

1/4 cup water

GARNISH

1 head Romaine lettuce, shredded

1 lemon, coarsely sliced

1. Make the salsa: Mix together the tomatoes, coriander, jalapeño peppers, and onion in a large bowl.

2. Preheat the oven to 350 degrees F.

3. Squeeze the juice of the lemon over the snapper filets to moisten them and let stand for a few minutes. Season with salt and pepper.

4. Make the rice: Sauté the onion and garlic in the vegetable oil in a large saucepan over medium heat. Rinse the rice well under very hot water and drain it. Add the rice to the pan and sauté until golden. Strain out the excess oil. Add the chicken stock to the pan and simmer, covered, for 15 to 20 minutes. Season with salt.

5. Meanwhile, on a lightly oiled large baking pan, arrange the filets, skin side down. Spoon the salsa generously over the fish, making a mound about 1/2 inch high and maintaining the shape of the filets. Pour the water among the filets. Bake for 10 to 12 minutes.

6. To serve, set the rice in the middle of a platter, top with the snapper and salsa, and garnish with the shredded lettuce and lemon slices.

SERVES 4

Every day seems like a party amid Zarela's collection of fanciful Mexican crafts and artifacts. Surrounded by oversized guava, kiwi, and passion fruit, you can sip strawberry margaritas and watch the guitar players, who wear colorful sombreros. Its talented chef, Zarela Martinez, inventively reinterprets classic Mexican dishes to create wondrous delicacies. Her signature dish, red snapper hash from Tampico, is full of heady aromatic spices and silky pieces of red snapper. Flavorful Ceylon cinnamon heightens the taste of the hash.

RED SNAPPER HASH

ZARELA

8 tablespoons sweet butter

6 large garlic cloves, peeled and finely minced

6–7 scallions, white and green parts, minced

3 medium ripe red tomatoes, chopped (2 1/2 cups)

3 fresh jalapeño or serrano peppers, tops trimmed, not seeded

1 1/2 teaspoons Ceylon cinnamon, freshly ground

1/2 teaspoon ground cloves

2 teaspoons ground cumin

1 teaspoon salt

2 1/2 pounds red snapper filets, skinned and cut into 4 pieces, all bones removed

GARNISH

1/2 pound corn tortillas or tortilla chips

1 lime, cut into thin round slices

1. In a large nonstick skillet, melt 4 tablespoons of the butter over medium heat. When the foam subsides, sauté half of the minced garlic for 1 minute, stirring constantly.

2. Add the scallions and cook for 1 minute longer, stirring. Add the tomatoes, peppers, spices, and salt and continue cooking for approximately 5 minutes, stirring often until the sauce thickens slightly.

3. Cut the fish filets in half and place them in the skillet with the tomato mixture. Over low heat, poach the fish, uncovered, until the meat turns opaque, approximately 1 minute, pressing the fish down into the mixture with a spatula. Turn the fish with the spatula and poach on the other side for an additional minute. Let the fish cool in the skillet. Shred the fish with your fingertips, making sure to remove any remaining bones.

4. In another large skillet, heat the remaining 4 tablespoons butter over medium heat until hot and bubbling. Sauté the remaining garlic for 1 minute, stirring. Add the shredded fish and sauce and cook until heated through.

5. Serve the red snapper hash with corn tortillas or tortilla chips. Garnish with lime slices.

SERVES 4

SWORDFISH WITH LEMON AND CAPERS

GIAMBELLI 50

four 6-ounce swordfish steaks, center cut,
   1/2 inch thick
1/2 cup flour for dredging
1/2 cup corn oil
salt and white pepper to taste
1/4 cup capers
juice of 2 freshly squeezed lemons

1/2 cup dry white wine
1/2 cup Light Chicken Stock (page 203)
2 tablespoons sweet butter

GARNISH
2 tablespoons chopped Italian parsley

The recipe for this simple yet tasty sautéed swordfish originated in Sicily, where the freshest seafood and capers abound. The delicate lemon and white wine sauce, perfumed with capers, perfectly complements the meaty swordfish steaks, creating a satisfying main course for any season.

1. Rinse the fish and pat dry. Dredge the fish in the flour and shake off the excess.

2. Heat the corn oil in a sauté pan until very hot. Season the swordfish with salt and pepper and cook until golden on both sides, 3 to 4 minutes. Discard excess oil.

3. Rinse the capers and then add them to the sauté pan with the fish, along with the lemon juice, white wine, and chicken stock. Add the butter and simmer, covered, until the sauce thickens and absorbs the flavor of the capers, approximately 5 minutes. If the sauce thickens too much, add more stock and reduce the sauce a little more.

4. To serve, arrange the fish on plates and spoon the sauce over the top. Garnish with the chopped parsley.

SERVES 4

This firm and tasty grilled tuna combines the sweetness of mango with the crunchiness of jícama. The crisp tortillas with their bold-flavored toppings exemplify Chef Bobby Flay's whimsical, colorful presentations. Chef Flay excels in presenting foods indigenous to the Southwest, giving them his own personal twist.

GRILLED TUNA TOSTADA WITH BLACK BEAN MANGO SALSA AND AVOCADO VINAIGRETTE

MESA GRILL

BLACK BEAN MANGO SALSA

1 cup black beans

1 cup peeled, diced mango

1 red onion, peeled and diced

1 jalapeño pepper, diced

$^1/_2$ cup chopped cilantro

$^1/_2$ cup fresh lime juice

4 tablespoons olive oil

salt and freshly ground white pepper to taste

AVOCADO VINAIGRETTE

$^1/_2$ avocado, peeled

$^1/_2$ jalapeño pepper

2 tablespoons chopped red onion

4 tablespoons fresh lime juice

1 teaspoon sugar

kosher salt and freshly ground pepper to taste

1 cup olive oil

3 cups vegetable oil

6 flour tortillas, 4 inches in diameter

6 loins of fresh tuna, 4 ounces each

GARNISH

$^1/_4$ cup julienned, peeled jícama

6 slices avocado

6 tablespoons chopped chives

3 tablespoons seeded, chopped red bell pepper

1. Make the black bean mango salsa: Cook the black beans, uncovered, for 45 minutes in 1$^1/_2$ cups boiling water. Drain. Combine the mango, red onion, jalapeño pepper, cilantro, lime juice, and olive oil in a bowl and mix well with the cooked beans. Season with salt and pepper to taste.

2. Make the avocado vinaigrette: In a blender or food processor, blend the avocado, jalapeño pepper, red onion, lime juice, sugar, and salt and pepper to taste until smooth. With the blender still on, slowly add the olive oil, allowing the vinaigrette to emulsify.

3. In a saucepan, heat the vegetable oil until hot. Add the tortillas and deep-fry them until they turn golden brown and the surface of the tortillas bubbles. Drain on paper towels.

4. Season the tuna with kosher salt and pepper, brush with olive oil, and slice each loin into 6 pieces. Place on a well-oiled grill and cook on both sides until rare or medium rare.

5. To serve, layer the ingredients in this order: (1) jícama, (2) 1 flour tortilla, (3) a thin layer of black bean mango salsa, (4) the grilled tuna, and (5) a thin slice of avocado. Garnish with chives and chopped red pepper and drizzle avocado vinaigrette in a zigzag pattern around the plate.

SERVES 6

The key to these exotically flavored tuna mignons is the caramelization that occurs during the searing process and the use of the finest sushi-grade tuna. Accompanied by puréed chive potatoes and a sauce of chive butter and soy sauce, this dish exemplifies the masterful and innovative cooking at Tropica. It is easy to understand why this food has been called exhilarating.

SEARED TUNA WITH POTATO PUREE AND CHIVE SAUCE

TROPICA

POTATO LATTICES (OPTIONAL)
1 Idaho potato, peeled
3 tablespoons olive oil
pinch of kosher salt
pinch of freshly ground white pepper
3 tablespoons sweet butter, melted

MARINADE
^{1}/$_2$ cup soy sauce
^{1}/$_4$ cup ketjap (*thick Indonesian sweet soy sauce*)
1 tablespoon sambal oelek (*mash of preserved peppers*), or chili paste
^{1}/$_2$ teaspoon lemongrass powder (*sereh powder*)
^{1}/$_4$ teaspoon ground white pepper
3 teaspoons extra-virgin olive oil
3 garlic cloves, peeled and sliced
3 teaspoons roughly chopped cilantro leaves

20 ounces clean, finest grade tuna loin, cut into 4 mignons

CHIVE BUTTER
3 bunches chives, chopped
^{1}/$_2$ bunch Italian flat-leaf parsley
2 sticks unsalted Plugrá butter, softened
juice of ^{1}/$_2$ lemon
2 tablespoons kosher salt

POTATO PUREE
3 large Idaho potatoes, peeled and cut into 3 pieces
2 cups warm cream

2 tablespoons hot water
2 teaspoons Japanese soy sauce

1 tablespoon olive oil

GARNISH
1 red bell pepper, seeded and finely diced
1 bunch chive sticks

(recipe continues on page 152)

1. Make the potato lattices (optional): Preheat the oven to 375 degrees F. Thinly slice the potato vertically with a *mandoline*. Then cut the pieces into ¹/₈-inch strips. In a small bowl, combine the olive oil, kosher salt, and white pepper. Coat the potato strips with the mixture, then baste with the melted butter. Place the strips directly on a nonstick baking pan in 4 parallel lines, then top with 4 parallel lines perpendicular to the first 4 lines. Bake (a convection oven, if available, is preferable) until the strips are browned, approximately 10 minutes. Remove the potato lattices to a dry towel and reserve.

2. Make the marinade: Mix together the soy sauce, *ketjap*, chili paste, lemongrass powder, ground white pepper, olive oil, garlic cloves, and cilantro in a large bowl. Add the tuna mignons and marinate for 20 minutes to 1 hour.

3. Make the chive butter: Place the chives, parsley, and butter in a food processor and blend the mixture until a smooth green color throughout. Add lemon juice and kosher salt. Refrigerate in a nonreactive glass or metal bowl, covered with plastic wrap, for 15 minutes.

4. Make the potato purée: Place the potatoes in a pot, cover with cold water, and add 1 tablespoon salt. Bring to a boil and simmer until the potatoes almost disintegrate. Drain the potatoes. Return them to the warm pot to allow excess moisture to evaporate. Then place in a warm oven for 2 to 3 minutes.

5. Pour half the warm cream into a medium saucepan and place a food mill over it. Mill the potatoes and then mash them with the cream using a rubber spatula. (You may not use all of the cream, depending on the moisture in the potatoes. If the potatoes are too stiff, add extra cream.) Season with kosher salt and freshly ground white pepper. Stir the potato mixture with the spatula. Add one-third of the chive butter to the potatoes and incorporate well. The potato mixture should be stirred over the warm stove even though the heat is extinguished.

6. In a nonreactive (nonaluminum) pan, place the remaining chive butter with the 2 tablespoons hot water, and cook on the stove, swirling, until incorporated. Season with salt and and freshly ground white pepper. Stir in the Japanese soy sauce.

7. Preheat the oven to 400 degrees F.

8. In a cast-iron skillet, heat 1 tablespoon olive oil until very hot. Shake off the excess marinade from the tuna and cook the fish, using tongs, making sure that all sides of the fish are seared. Place the skillet in the oven and cook an additional 5 to 10 minutes, depending on desired doneness. (The chef advises rare to medium rare.) Let the fish rest for a few minutes and then slice each of the 4 mignons into 4 pieces.

9. To serve, place 3 tablespoons of the potato purée in the center of each plate. Overlap the 4 slices of tuna and drizzle the chive-butter sauce around the fish. Garnish with the diced red pepper and 3 chive sticks around the potato purée, leaning the sticks across one another to form a triangle. Place the potato lattices (optional) vertically in the potato purée.

HINTS FROM THE CHEF: Many of the ingredients in this recipe can be obtained in specialty stores, particularly Indian spice shops. Plugrá, a European-style butter from France ("*plus gras*" means more fat) is available in some specialty shops and since it is richer and more flavorful than the common American variety, it is particularly good in sauces and desserts.

SERVES 4

DESSERTS

Biscotti, *classic Italian cookies served with* Vin Santo, *are traditionally prepared with hazelnuts, almonds, and wheat flour. Mesa Grill reimagines them as a Southwestern treat, using all-American ingredients: pecans, pistachios, and yellow and blue cornmeal.*

BLUE CORN BISCOTTI

MESA GRILL

2³/4 cups all-purpose flour

1¹/4 cups sugar

2 tablespoons coarse yellow cornmeal

6 tablespoons blue cornmeal

1¹/2 teaspoons baking powder

¹/2 teaspoon salt

¹/2 cup pistachios, shelled and whole

¹/2 cup pecan pieces

8 tablespoons sweet butter, softened

2 eggs

2 tablespoons anisette

1. Preheat the oven to 350 degrees F.

2. On the slowest mixer speed, combine all the dry ingredients, including the pistachios and pecans. Slowly add the softened butter in bits, mixing well. Add the eggs and the anisette and knead for approximately 4 minutes.

3. Press the dough into logs 3¹/2 inches wide by 15 inches long by 1 inch thick. Do not roll the dough since rolling creates air pockets. Make sure that the ends are the same thickness as the middle. Place the logs on a nonstick baking sheet and bake for 40 minutes. Let cool.

4. Slice the logs into ¹/3-inch-thick pieces and bake again at 350 degrees F. for 8 minutes, until very lightly browned.

HINTS FROM THE CHEF: Pour the pistachios onto a flat surface before using so you can find and remove any hidden shells.

Coarse yellow cornmeal is preferred in this recipe as it has a strong flavor and a nice gritty texture.

YIELD: 24 BISCOTTI

CREME BRULEE

LE CIRQUE

4 cups heavy cream

1 vanilla bean

8 egg yolks

³/₄ cup granulated sugar

³/₄ cup light brown sugar

1. Preheat the oven to 300 degrees F.

2. In a saucepan over low heat, warm the cream and vanilla bean for 5 minutes.

3. In a bowl, whisk the egg yolks and granulated sugar. Stir the cream mixture gradually into the egg mixture and combine. Strain the custard into another bowl and skim off the bubbles.

4. Fill a roasting pan halfway with boiling water. Fill 8 ceramic 6- × 4¹/₂-inch oval custard dishes to the rim with the custard mixture and place them in the roasting pan. Cover the pan loosely with aluminum foil and bake for 1 to 1¹/₄ hours, until the custard is set but wiggles a little. Remove the custard dishes from the water bath and let cool. Cover each custard with plastic wrap and refrigerate for at least 3 hours or for as long as 2 days.

5. Just prior to serving, spread a thin layer of sifted brown sugar evenly over each custard with a knife. Melt the sugar either by applying the flame of a propane torch to the tops of the custards or by placing the custards on the middle rack in the broiler, 2 inches from the heat, for 30 seconds to 2 minutes, until the sugar is caramelized. Watch the custards closely to make sure the sugar does not burn.

NOTE: Vanilla extract should not be substituted for the vanilla bean. To remove the vanilla scrapings from the vanilla bean, slice the vanilla bean lengthwise and scrape out the beans with a sharp knife into the saucepan with the milk. For additional flavor, I recommend leaving the whole vanilla bean in the mixture, removing it prior to pouring the finished custard into the individual *crème brûlée* dishes.

SERVES 8

Rich and ethereal, this creamy-textured custard crystallized with light brown sugar is one of my favorite dinner party desserts because it makes an elegant presentation and can be prepared almost entirely in advance. Le Cirque's legendary crème brûlée exemplifies the wonderful indulgences of its culinary repertoire.

This French toast, which is made with brioche and topped with the most tender caramelized apples, will be the centerpiece of any breakfast or dessert menu. It reflects the lightness and simple cuisine of the acclaimed chef Jean-Georges Vongerichten, who prior to coming to the United States apprenticed at such renowned three-star Michelin restaurants as L'Oasis in Cannes and Paul Bocuse in Lyons.

BRIOCHE PERDUE TOPPED WITH CARAMELIZED APPLES

J O J O

1 loaf Brioche (page 194)

LAIT DE POULE
1¼ cups heavy cream
½ cup milk
⅔ cup sugar
1 tablespoon dark rum
5 egg yolks

CREME ANGLAISE
1 vanilla bean
2 cups cream
2 cups milk
½ cup sugar
5 egg yolks

2 Golden Delicious apples
5 tablespoons Clarified Butter
  (page 196)

1. Cut the brioche loaf into ¾-inch slices.

2. Make the *lait de poule*: In a large bowl, whisk together the heavy cream, milk, sugar, rum, and egg yolks. Soak the brioche in the mixture for 10 minutes until the liquid permeates the bread.

3. Make the *crème anglaise*: Split the vanilla bean lengthwise and remove the scrapings. Combine the cream, milk, scrapings and vanilla bean, and half the sugar in a saucepan. Heat the mixture until it boils. In a bowl, blend the egg yolks and the remaining sugar until smooth. Temper the egg yolk mixture by adding a little of the hot cream mixture to the bowl. Pour the tempered egg yolk-sugar mixture into the hot cream mixture and cook over low heat, stirring constantly, until it lightly coats the back of a spoon.

4. Peel and core the apples, cut them in half vertically, then cut in half again. Heat 3 tablespoons of clarified butter in a saucepan and sauté the apples over low heat until browned.

5. While the apples are cooking, melt 1 tablespoon of the clarified butter in a 10-inch nonstick pan until hot but not smoking. Add the brioche and cook until browned. (You should be able to cook about 2 or 3 slices at a time.) After each batch, wipe out the pan, add more clarified butter, and repeat the process.

6. To serve, place 1 slice of brioche in the center of each plate and top with warm caramelized apples. Spoon *crème anglaise* around the plate. Serve immediately.

SERVES 4

Chef David Burke's masterful use of French cooking techniques creates dazzling American sensations. Full of gastronomic surprises and drama, this extravagant, moist, spiced carrot cake soufflé exudes a luscious, creamy confection.

WARM CREAM CHEESE AND CARROT CAKE SOUFFLE

PARK AVENUE CAFE

CREAM CHEESE PASTRY CREAM

1 pound cream cheese

$^1/_2$ cup sugar

3 egg yolks

CARROT CAKE MIXTURE

1 egg

1 tablespoon brown sugar

2 tablespoons sugar

3 tablespoons vegetable oil

2 tablespoons honey

$^1/_8$ teaspoon salt

$^3/_4$ cup all-purpose flour

$^1/_2$ teaspoon ground cinnamon

$^1/_2$ teaspoon freshly grated nutmeg

$^1/_4$ teaspoon clove

$^1/_2$ teaspoon allspice

$^1/_4$ teaspoon baking soda

$^1/_8$ teaspoon baking powder

$^2/_3$ cup shredded carrots

$^1/_8$ cup chopped walnuts

$^1/_8$ cup raisins

SOUFFLE BATTER

1 cup cream cheese pastry cream

3 egg yolks

3 egg whites

$^1/_2$ cup sugar

LIGHT CREAM CHEESE SAUCE

1 cup cream cheese

$^3/_4$ cup sugar

1 cup freshly squeezed orange juice

2 sheets prestretched phyllo dough or strudel leaves

$^1/_2$ cup Clarified Butter (page 196)

GARNISH

1 pint raspberries

4 navel oranges, peeled and divided into segments

1 bunch mint

1. Make the cream cheese pastry cream: Heat the cream cheese and half the sugar over low heat, stirring occasionally, until the cream cheese melts and no lumps remain. While the cream cheese is melting, stir the yolks and the remaining sugar into the cream cheese and cook over low heat, whisking until thick. Cool, cover with plastic wrap, and refrigerate until ready to use.

2. Make the carrot cake mixture: With an electric mixer, whip the egg and sugars on high speed until the mixture rises to a mousselike consistency. Then, at high speed, gradually add the vegetable oil and honey until both are incorporated. Add the dry ingredients and spices, and mix by hand until the flour is no longer visible. Add the shredded carrots, chopped walnuts, and raisins and mix until evenly distributed.

3. Make the soufflé batter: Mix together the cream cheese pastry cream and egg yolks until no lumps are visible. In an electric mixer bowl, beat the egg whites until soft peaks form. Then slowly incorporate the sugar until firm peaks (meringue) form, approximately 10 minutes. Fold the meringue into the yolk and cream mixture.

4. Make the light cream cheese sauce: Warm the cream cheese and sugar in a saucepan over low heat, whisking occasionally. Add orange juice and continue cooking until emulsified. Strain the mixture. Reserve.

5. Preheat the oven to 425 degrees F.

6. Assemble the soufflé: Line a baking pan with parchment and brush with clarified butter. Place eight 4-inch metal rings on top of the buttered parchment. Place a sheet of the phyllo dough on a clean countertop and brush with clarified butter. Cover the phyllo dough with a second piece of phyllo dough and brush with clarified butter. Using a 5-inch metal ring and a sharp paring knife, cut out eight 5-inch rounds of phyllo dough. Place a round of dough, buttered side down, in the bottom of each metal ring on the baking sheet. (The dough will come up the sides a little and thus prevent the cake from seeping out the bottom.) Brush the top of the dough with clarified butter. Cut the remaining phyllo dough into eight $12^3/_4$- $\times$ 1-inch strips. Brush each strip with clarified butter. Place 1 strip around the inside edge of each ring, buttered side toward the ring. Fill a pastry bag fitted with a #6 tip with the carrot cake mixture and pipe 2 tablespoons of the mixture into the bottom of each ring, spreading it evenly around the bottom. Top the carrot cake mixture with 3 tablespoons of the soufflé batter and even out the top as much as possible. Using a paring knife, cut a square around each mold in the parchment so that you will be able to lift the soufflés off the pan more easily when you are ready to unmold. Bake for 7 to 10 minutes.

7. To serve: Unmold the soufflés by placing each one in the middle of a dinner plate and lifting the metal ring, sliding a knife between the soufflé and the parchment to remove the paper. Spoon the light cream cheese sauce around each soufflé and place 4 or 5 raspberries and 4 orange segments in the sauce. Top each soufflé with a mint sprig.

SERVES 8

Although muffins are not typically a dessert, they remain an American classic. Sprinkled with a topping of light and dark sugars, these lightly textured fruit muffins are moistened with ripe bananas that add a welcome natural sweetness. Sarabeth Levine's preserves, containing the tastiest, juiciest chunks of strawberries and peaches, accompany these muffins and are so popular that they are marketed nationwide.

BLUEBERRY-BANANA MUFFINS WITH STRAWBERRY-PEACH PRESERVES

SARABETH'S KITCHEN

STRAWBERRY-PEACH
   PRESERVES
2¹/₂ pounds peaches, peeled, pitted, and
   cut into 1-inch chunks
2 pints strawberries, hulled and halved
³/₄ cup fresh lemon juice
6 cups sugar

MUFFINS
¹/₂ cup (1 stick) sweet butter, at room
   temperature
³/₈ cup light brown sugar, packed
1 cup granulated sugar
¹/₃ cup eggs, beaten (approximately 3
   eggs)

¹/₂ tablespoon vanilla
3 cups unbleached flour
1 tablespoon baking powder
¹/₈ teaspoon salt
1 cup milk
1¹/₂ cups heavy cream
2 bananas, peeled and sliced
1 cup blueberries, washed and drained

CRUMBS
¹/₂ cup (1 stick) butter
¹/₄ cup white sugar
¹/₄ cup brown sugar, packed
1 cup all-purpose flour

1. Make the strawberry-peach preserves: In a medium saucepan, cook the peaches and strawberries with the lemon juice over medium heat for approximately 15 minutes, stirring from time to time. Add the sugar, stirring occasionally until it dissolves, and cook an additional 5 minutes. Over medium-high heat, bring the mixture to a boil. Reduce the heat and simmer for approximately 1 hour, stirring occasionally, until the mixture thickens and holds its shape when placed on a cold plate. Cool well. Pour into three 1-pint sterilized preserve jars and cover the top of each with a thin layer of melted paraffin.

2. Preheat the oven to 400 degrees F. Butter the muffin tins well, making sure to grease the sections between the cups.

3. In a large mixing bowl, cream the butter and sugars until light and fluffy. Add the eggs, one at a time, beating well after each addition so that the mixture is very light. Beat in the vanilla.

4. In a mixing bowl, combine the flour, baking powder, and salt. Toss until combined.

5. Combine the milk and cream in a bowl. Alternate adding the dry ingredients and the liquid ingredients to the butter mixture until the batter is well combined. Fold in the bananas and blueberries.

6. Make the crumb topping: In a small saucepan over low heat, melt the butter and mix in the white and brown sugars. Incorporate the flour and mix well.

7. Place ½ cup of the batter into each muffin tin using a number 20 ice cream scoop. Sprinkle each muffin with a little of the crumb topping. Bake in the lower third of the oven for 25 to 30 minutes, or until the muffins are golden brown and well rounded. Halfway through the baking time, rotate the muffin pan in the oven so that the muffins cook evenly. Remove the muffin tin from the oven to a rack to cool for 10 to 15 minutes before removing the muffins. Serve with the preserves.

YIELD: 12 MUFFINS

While scones with black currants conjure up images of clotted cream and thatched cottages, they remain a venerable Old World tradition at The Palm Court's legendary tea service. High tea at the Plaza rivals even the grandest of England and Scotland. This coveted recipe has been requested by patrons around the world.

SCONES WITH BLACK CURRANTS

THE PALM COURT AT THE PLAZA

3/4 cup dry black currants

1 stick sweet butter, softened

1/2 cup sugar

2 jumbo or 3 small eggs

2 cups cake flour

1 1/2 cups bread flour

1 3/4 tablespoons baking powder

1 cup heavy cream

1 teaspoon vanilla

EGG WASH

2 eggs

1 tablespoon water

pinch of salt

1. Place the currants in a small bowl, cover them with water, and let them soak for 1 hour.

2. Cream the butter and sugar with an electric mixer set on medium speed for 5 minutes. Beat in the eggs, one at a time, blending well after each.

3. In a large bowl, sift together the cake flour, bread flour, and baking powder. Stir the dry ingredients into the egg mixture, beating well with an electric mixer until incorporated. Slowly pour in the cream, add the vanilla and currants, and mix until all the ingredients are incorporated. The dough should be sticky and a little rough and almost firm. Allow the dough to rest for 15 minutes before rolling it out.

4. Roll out the dough with a rolling pin on a well-floured surface to a $^3/_4$-inch thickness. Dust the dough well with flour and press down on it with your hands, starting in the middle, to form a square shape. Let the dough relax by picking up the edges with your fingers so that it contracts. Cut circles out of the dough, using a $2^1/_4$-inch round biscuit cutter or round metal ring, and place the rounds on a baking sheet lined with baking parchment. Dust off the excess flour and let the scones rest for 1 hour in a cool place.

5. Preheat the oven to 375 degrees F.

6. Make the egg wash: Lightly beat the eggs, water, and salt together.

7. Brush the scones with the wash. Bake for approximately 25 minutes, or until the scones are golden.

HINTS FROM THE CHEF: If you let the scone mixture rest prior to baking, the scones will have more body. After the dough is cut into the shape of scones, it can be frozen for up to 1 week. Bread flour has more gluten, a protein-building material, than regular flour and therefore is preferable. The use of both bread and cake flours gives these scones their unique taste. However, if bread flour is unavailable, use a good quality all-purpose flour, such as Gold Medal or White Lily. You may substitute raisins, almond slivers, or chocolate chips for the currants.

YIELD: 20 SCONES

TIRAMISU

P R I M A V E R A

1 cup brewed espresso, cooled

2 tablespoons brandy

18 hardened Italian ladyfingers

3 eggs, separated

3 tablespoons fine sugar

$^1/_2$ pound mascarpone cheese

$^1/_2$ cup bittersweet chocolate, finely
 chopped

G A R N I S H

$^1/_2$ pint fresh raspberries

6 mint leaves

*This delightful confection of
ladyfingers macerated in espresso
and brandy perfectly complements
the shredded chocolate topping.
This is* tiramisù *at its finest,
particularly for those, like myself,
who prefer a less creamy texture.
Some recipes use Kahlua and rum,
but I prefer this more subtle
version.*

1. In a large bowl, combine the espresso and the brandy. One by one, immerse the ladyfingers in the coffee mixture, leaving each submerged for just less than a minute. Arrange half of the ladyfingers on the bottom of a shallow 3-quart serving dish. The ladyfingers should be touching one another.

2. In a mixing bowl, beat the egg yolks with the sugar until fluffy. In another bowl, beat the egg whites until they are stiff and fold in the *mascarpone* cheese. Gently combine the two egg mixtures.

3. Cover the ladyfingers with half the egg mixture and sprinkle them with half the chocolate. Top with the remaining dipped ladyfingers and add another layer of the egg mixture. Sprinkle with the remaining chocolate. Cover with aluminum foil and refrigerate for 1 hour before serving.

4. To serve, scoop the *tiramisù* onto plates, using a serving spoon to create 2 ovals. You may also present individual portions of *tiramisù* in large goblets or other decorative glassware, following the procedure above for assembling and refrigerating. Garnish with fresh raspberries and mint leaves.

N O T E :   You should only use the finest imported chocolate, such as Le Nôtre, Callebaut, and Valrhona, often available at Williams-Sonoma, P.O. Box 7456, San Francisco, CA 94120-7456 (1-800-541-2233); or Dean & DeLuca, 560 Broadway, New York, NY 10012 (1-800-221-7714); or other specialty stores. Buy fresh ladyfingers from a bakery or, if unavailable, buy an imported rather than a domestic variety from your grocery store. Imported *mascarpone* cheese is also preferable. Make sure not to overwhelm the ladyfingers with too much brandy since the *mascarpone* is also sweet.

S E R V E S   6

For raspberry lovers like me, this English pudding steeped, filled, and topped with the sweetest, ripest raspberries is the ultimate summer treat. Resembling an English currant trifle cake, this creation, served with a dollop of whipped cream or crème fraîche, *is sure to draw raves from your dinner guests. The pudding can be made equally well by alternating layers of raspberries and blackberries or any seasonal berries.*

RASPBERRY SUMMER PUDDING

THE FOUR SEASONS

6 pints fresh raspberries

³/4 cup sugar

1 pound white bread, sliced and crusts removed

2 tablespoons raspberry jam or raspberry preserves, melted with a tablespoon of water

GARNISH

¹/4 cup heavy cream, whipped, or ¹/2 cup Crème Fraîche (page 196), optional

4 fresh mint leaves

candied violets, optional

1. Lightly rinse 4 pints of the raspberries. Place them in a large bowl with the sugar and mix with a wooden spatula until the berries are just crushed. Macerate the berries, stirring them occasionally, until they are half liquefied. (The sugar will draw the juice out of the berries.)

2. Line the bottom of a round 6- × 2-inch cake pan with a sheet of plastic wrap, leaving enough to cover the top of the pudding later on. Neatly spoon a very thin layer of berries (just enough to coat) over the bottom of the pan. Top with a layer of bread that fits together so neatly that it looks like the pieces of a puzzle. Continue layering until you have 3 layers of bread alternating with 4 layers of raspberries. All the layers of raspberries, except the top and the bottom layers, should be the same thickness as the bread. (There may be a little raspberry-sugar mixture left over.) Cover the top of the cake with the reserved plastic wrap, then place a weight on top. Refrigerate overnight.

3. Knock the pan on a table to loosen the pudding and then unmold it carefully onto a 6-inch round cardboard or cake plate. Remove the plastic wrap.

4. Mix the melted raspberry jam or raspberry preserves with the remaining 2 pints berries, taking care not to bruise the raspberries. Cover the top of the pudding artfully with the berries, arranging them in concentric circles.

5. To serve, slice generously and garnish with whipped cream or *crème fraîche*, fresh mint leaves, and candied violets.

SERVES 6

This warming, cinnamon-flavored Norman tart, with its sumptuous crème pâtissière *and aromatic Red Delicious apples, remains one of my favorites. Perhaps the touch of Calvados, the noble apple brandy of Normandy, lifts this tart into the sublime and makes it one of the stars of La Côte Basque's haute cuisine.*

TARTE NORMANDE

LA COTE BASQUE

10 ounces *Puff Pastry (page 202)*

4 tablespoons sweet butter

5 large Red Delicious apples, cored, peeled, and diced

3 ¹/₂ tablespoons sugar

1 teaspoon cinnamon

2 tablespoons Calvados

CREME PATISSIERE

5 egg yolks

3 ¹/₄ tablespoons sugar

1 tablespoon cornstarch

1 cup milk

1 sheet gelatin, softened in 1 cup of cold water

2 egg whites

GARNISH
granulated sugar

1. Preheat the oven to 350 degrees F.

2. Thinly roll out the puff pastry dough on a floured surface. Line a 10-inch round tart pan with a removable bottom with the dough, using your fingers to press it against the bottom and sides of the pan.

3. In a large sauté pan over medium heat, melt the butter and add the apples. Cook for 5 minutes, then add the sugar, cinnamon, and Calvados. When cool, place the apple mixture in the pastry shell and bake for 40 minutes. Remove the pan from the oven and let it cool. Remove the bottom of the pan and place the tart on a cardboard round the size of the pan; replace the ring around the tart.

4. Make the *crème pâtissière*: In a large bowl, beat the egg yolks well with the sugar until thick and lemon colored. Then stir in the cornstarch. In a large saucepan, bring the milk to a boil. Pour half the milk into a separate saucepan and whisk the egg mixture into it for 1 minute over low heat. Then add the other half of the boiled milk and whisk until well combined. Remove the pan from the heat and add the softened gelatin and whisk lightly. In a separate bowl, whip the egg whites until stiff peaks form. Fold the egg whites into the egg and milk mixture and let cool.

5. Pour the *crème pâtissière* over the apples so that the custard is approximately 1 inch thick and sits up a little higher than the rim of the pan. Flatten the top evenly with a spatula and discard any excess *crème pâtissière*. Refrigerate the tart.

6. When cold, generously sprinkle sugar on top. Caramelize the sugar by placing the tart under the broiler for 1 or 2 minutes.

N O T E :   If you don't have a blowtorch, the easiest method for caramelizing the sugar without damaging the tart is to melt 1 cup sugar in a saucepan stirring constantly. When completely melted, immediately pour the sugar over the top of the cake.

S E R V E S   8

In a city where the only constant is change, two things stand apart from the flow of time: Gage & Tollner's Victorian interior and its timeless blackberry cobbler. Cobblers were brought to Virginia by the first English settlers in the early 1600s. This fruit cobbler, accented with an orange-scented nutmeg sauce, is equally delicious made with blueberries, apples, or juicy peaches.

BLACKBERRY COBBLER

GAGE & TOLLNER

$^1/_2$ *orange, peel only*

PIE PASTRY
2 cups unbleached all-purpose flour
1 teaspoon salt
12 tablespoons firmly chilled sweet
   butter, cut into bits
$^1/_4$ *cup ice water*

1 cup sugar
1 pint ripe blackberries

NUTMEG SAUCE
$^2/_3$ *cup sugar*
pinch of salt
2 teaspoons cornstarch
$^1/_4$ *teaspoon freshly grated nutmeg*
1 cup boiling water
3 tablespoons brandy

1. Dry a 2-inch piece of orange peel on a rack for several days at room temperature.

2. Make the pie pastry: Place the flour, salt, and all but 2 tablespoons of butter, cut into bits, in a mixing bowl. Blend well with your fingertips until a grainy texture is achieved. Add the ice water and mix quickly, shaping the dough into a ball. Dust it lightly with flour and shape it into a flat disc. Wrap in wax paper and refrigerate for 30 minutes.

3. Divide the dough into 2 pieces, one slightly larger than the other. On a lightly floured surface, roll out the larger piece of dough to fit an 8-inch pie pan, 2 inches deep. The dough will be about $^1/_4$ inch thick. Place the dough in the pan, sprinkle it with a small amount of sugar, and refrigerate for several hours.

4. Roll out the remaining piece of dough and cut it into strips that are approximately the length of the pie plate (you should have at least 8 strips). (Reserve to make the latticework on top of the pie.) Wrap the strips in wax paper and refrigerate. If you are making the pie dough ahead of time, be sure to let the dough strips rest at room temperature for $1^1/_2$ hours before using them.

5. Preheat the oven to 450 degrees F.

6. Sprinkle half the remaining sugar over the pie shell and fill with the blackberries. Sprinkle the blackberries with the remaining sugar and 2 tablespoons butter, cut into bits. Create a lattice top by first stretching 4 strips of dough across the pie and then weaving 4 strips perpendicular to the first 4 strips. Dip your fingers in cold water and seal the strips to the rim of the pie shell.

7. Bake the pie on the middle rack of the oven for 10 minutes at 450 degrees F., then lower the heat to 425 degrees F. and bake an additional 35 minutes.

8. Make the nutmeg sauce: While the cobbler is baking, place the sugar, salt, cornstarch, and nutmeg in a saucepan and cover with the boiling water. Add the 2-inch piece of dried orange peel and gently boil over medium heat for 12 minutes. Remove the pan from the heat and stir in the brandy. Remove the orange peel just before serving.

9. To serve, cut the cobbler into slices and spoon warm nutmeg sauce over each slice. Top with whipped cream or ice cream.

S E R V E S   4

Brooklyn's River Café provides not only a stunning panoramic view of the harbor and Manhattan's financial district but also dazzling culinary presentations. This stir-fried fruit candied in jasmine-scented caramel and topped with homemade ginger ice cream reflects the subtle influences of Japanese cooking on American cuisine.

STIR-FRIED FRUIT WITH GINGER ICE CREAM

THE RIVER CAFE

GINGER ICE CREAM
1 quart milk
1 cup cream
2-inch piece of fresh ginger, peeled and finely grated
4 tablespoons corn syrup
8 egg yolks
1 cup sugar

JASMINE CARAMEL
2 cups sugar
$^1/_2$ cup water
2 cups strong-brewed jasmine tea

2 tablespoons grapeseed oil
1 cup cantaloupe, thinly sliced and cut into $1^1/_2$-inch cubes
1 cup fresh pineapple, sliced into $1^1/_2$-inch cubes
$^1/_2$ cup blackberries
$^1/_2$ cup raspberries
$^1/_2$ cup blueberries
4 tablespoons Grand Marnier

GARNISH
4 mint leaves

1. Make the ginger ice cream: In a large copper saucepan, bring the milk, cream, ginger, and corn syrup to a boil. Let the mixture sit off the heat for 15 minutes to infuse. In a mixing bowl, whip the egg yolks and sugar until they turn pale yellow. Bring the cream and milk back to a boil and temper the yolks and sugar mixture by slowly pouring the boiling cream mixture on top of it. Whisk constantly to bring the yolks to the same temperature as the cream. Return this yolk mixture to the copper saucepan and over low heat stir constantly with a wooden spoon until it is thick enough to coat the back of the spoon. Strain. Cool the mixture by placing the saucepan in a bowl filled with ice. When cool, pour it into an ice cream machine and freeze it according to the manufacturer's directions.

2. Make the jasmine caramel: Place the sugar in a saucepan over medium heat, stir in the $^1/_2$ cup water, and heat until the sugar caramelizes to a medium brown. Remove from the stove and add the infused tea a little at a time. Whisk carefully to avoid burning yourself with the steam.

3. Stir-fry the fruit: Heat the grapeseed oil in a wok. Add the cantaloupe and pineapple cubes and cook until slightly caramelized, approximately 2 to 3 minutes. Add the blackberries, raspberries, and blueberries and stir-fry gently for an additional 3 minutes. Add 4 tablespoons of the jasmine caramel and the Grand Marnier in the wok, stirring constantly.

4. To serve, arrange the fruit in large salad or soup bowls and top each portion with an oval scoop of ginger ice cream. Garnish with mint leaves and serve immediately.

SERVES 4

This dazzling fruit soup with a fish-shaped tuile cookie perched in the mango sorbet affords a refreshing quencher for a hot summer day. The colorful maceration of mango, papaya, kiwi, and passion fruit evokes the tropical exoticism of the islands.

TROPICAL FRUIT SOUP WITH MANGO SORBET

TROPICA

CANDIED ORANGE ZEST
1 large orange
$1/2$ cup sugar
$1/2$ cup water
2 tablespoons grenadine

SYRUP
$1/2$ cup water
$3/4$ cup sugar
zest of 1 orange, finely julienned
zest of $1/2$ lime, finely julienned
zest of 1 lemon, finely julienned

MANGO SORBET
1 cup water
1 cup sugar
10 ounces natural mango purée, canned
2 tablespoons fresh lime juice

TUILES (MAKES 10 COOKIES)
4 egg whites
1 cup plus 1 tablespoon sugar

5 tablespoons sweet butter, melted
$1/3$ cup plus 1 tablespoon all-purpose flour
1 vanilla bean, scraped

FRUIT SOUP
1 kiwi, peeled
$3/4$ mango, peeled
$1/8$ pineapple, peeled
$1/2$ papaya, peeled and cut into small dice
1 fresh passion fruit, peeled
$1/2$ bunch mint
4 stalks lemongrass
2 cinnamon sticks
8 cloves

GARNISH
confectioners' sugar
8 mint leaves, finely julienned

1. Make the candied orange zest: Peel off the orange rind, making sure to include a little white pith. Cut it into thin strips with a sharp knife or zester. Place it in a saucepan with water to cover and bring to a boil. Drain the excess water from the pan and set the rind aside. Add the sugar and water to the pan and cook over low heat for 5 minutes. Add the zest and bring the mixture to a boil. Remove the mixture to a small bowl, add the grenadine, and let sit at room temperature for 1 day. Remove the rind and drain it on a paper towel.

2. Make the syrup: Combine the water, sugar, and zests in a saucepan over medium heat. Bring the mixture to a boil, cool, and then refrigerate until ready to serve.

3. Make the mango sorbet: Place the water and sugar in a large saucepan over medium heat. Bring to a boil and simmer for 15 minutes. Cool. Pour the mango purée into a food processor and blend until very smooth. Pour the purée into a mixing bowl, add the sugar syrup, and mix. Add the lime juice and chill. Pour the mixture into an ice cream machine and make sorbet according to the manufacturer's directions. If an ice cream machine is unavailable, refrigerate the mixture for 1 hour in a metal ice-cube tray. Every 10 minutes stir the sorbet with a fork until ice crystals form. Scoop out the cubes and chill them in the freezer in an airtight container.

(recipe continues on next page)

4. Preheat the oven to 350 degrees F.

5. Make the *tuiles:* Place the egg whites in a mixer and using the paddle beat slowly on the first speed until soft peaks form. Slowly add the sugar and mix on a moderate speed until frothy, approximately 3 to 4 minutes. Gradually add the butter at the slowest speed, then add the flour tossed with the vanilla bean scrapings and mix until incorporated. Refrigerate for 1 hour to facilitate spreading the batter. Make a template or stencil to create the desired pattern (fish and palm trees work well). First, cut out a large circle from a flat plastic surface (try using a sour cream or yogurt container flattened open at the seams). Then cut your design out of the circle. Place the template on a well-buttered baking sheet or "pastry plaque" (nonstick flat pastry sheet) in a baking sheet and using a plastic spatula, thinly spread the batter over the template. Remove the template and repeat the process to make the desired number of *tuiles,* placing them one inch apart. Bake for 5 minutes, or until the edges have just begun to brown. Remove the *tuiles* immediately from the baking sheet and place on a flat surface.

6. Make the fruit soup: Cut the kiwi, mango, pineapple, papaya, and passion fruit into small cubes and macerate together in a bowl with the mint, lemongrass, cinnamon sticks, and cloves. Add the zests of orange, lime, and lemon. Let sit covered with plastic wrap for ¹/₂ hour.

7. To serve, remove the cinnamon sticks and cloves from the fruit and portion the fruit evenly among 4 bowls. Pour the syrup mixture into the bowls until each bowl is one-third full. Place the mango sorbet in the center in oval shapes. (Use an oval ice cream scoop or place 2 soup spoons in warm water and turn sorbet from one spoon to the other until desired shape is formed.) Dust the *tuiles* with powdered sugar and place 1 cookie in each scoop of sorbet. Sprinkle the sorbet with the mint and the candied orange zest.

HINTS FROM THE CHEF: Mango purée may be purchased at Indian grocery stores or other specialty shops. While fresh mangos can be used, the purée gives the sorbet a more intense flavor. Passion fruit sorbet may also be made with passion fruit purée, following the same procedure, but will require the addition of a small amount of sugar to taste to compensate for the tartness of the passion fruit.

SERVES 4

SPICED RICE CRISPIES TRUFFLES

THE RIVER CAFE

3/4 cup heavy cream

1/2 vanilla bean, scrapings and bean

2 inches ginger, peeled and chopped

1 clove

1/2 cinnamon stick

1/4 teaspoon grated nutmeg

1 3/4 pounds milk chocolate, chopped

2 tablespoons sweet butter, softened

1 1/4 cups Rice Crispies cereal (or puffed rice cereal)

These two regal confections demonstrate the River Café's approach to merging American ingredients with classic French techniques. A fanciful version of the French chocolate truffle adds Rice Crispies, providing a refreshing crunchiness to the creamy-textured chocolate. The orange caramels with slivers of almonds are elegant indeed.

1. In a medium copper saucepan, bring the heavy cream, vanilla bean and scrapings, ginger, clove, cinnamon stick, and nutmeg to a boil. Let the mixture sit at room temperature for 30 minutes so that the seasonings will infuse the cream, then bring the mixture back to a rapid boil.

2. Place 1 1/4 pounds of the milk chocolate in a medium bowl. Strain the infusion through a *chinois* over the chopped chocolate and let it set for 2 minutes. Stir the mixture with a whisk and whisk in the softened butter until the mixture is smooth. Cool, cover with plastic wrap, and refrigerate.

3. With your hands, roll the *ganache* into logs 1 inch thick × 6 inches long and place them on a marble board lightly dusted with confectioners' sugar. Roll each log out to approximately 12 inches long and 3/4 inch thick. Using a small paring knife, cut off 3/4-inch sections. Roll the pieces into balls with the palms of your hands. Place the truffles on baking pans lined with parchment and place in the freezer just until they set. (The recipe can be made in advance up to this point.)

4. Melt the remaining chocolate in the top portion of a double boiler until it reaches 115 degrees F. on a candy thermometer. (Do not cover the chocolate as water could condense on the lid and drop into the chocolate, causing it to seize.) Remove the chocolate from the heat and stir vigorously for a few seconds to cool.

5. Temper the chocolate: Pour one-third of the mixture onto a marble slab and using a small metal spatula, press the chocolate outward and then back toward the center (work the spatula in a figure eight configuration) for approximately 10 minutes, or until it thickens and has the consistency of paste. Add the cooled, tempered chocolate to the melted chocolate in the pan and mix until smooth. Rewarm over warm water for approximately 10 seconds.

6. Stir the Rice Crispies into the bowl of chocolate and dip the hardened truffles in it, making sure they are well coated. Transfer to a baking pan lined with parchment to set. If you are not serving the truffles immediately, cover with plastic wrap and refrigerate.

YIELD: 50 CANDIES

ORANGE CARAMEL

THE RIVER CAFE

1/4 pound almonds, peeled and sliced	*1/4 cup honey*
1 cup heavy cream	*grated zest of 3 oranges*
1 cup sugar	*2 tablespoons sweet butter*
1/2 cup corn syrup	*1/2 pound milk chocolate*
	2 1/2 ounces dark chocolate

1. Preheat the oven to 350 degrees F.

2. Place the almonds in a dry baking pan and toast them in the oven for 10 minutes, or until they start to color.

3. Place the cream, sugar, corn syrup, and honey in a 4-quart copper saucepan. Sprinkle the orange zest over the mixture and bring to a boil, cooking until a candy thermometer reaches 240 degrees F. (The mixture should be a rich caramel color.) Promptly remove from the stove and whisk in the butter. Stir in the toasted almonds with a wooden spoon.

4. Place a square bottomless cake pan on a baking sheet lined with parchment. Pour the caramel mixture into the ring or pan so that it is approximately 3/4 inch high and flatten it with a metal spatula. When the mixture has cooled and hardened, cut it into 3/4-inch squares, making sure to trim the edges so they are perfectly even. Cover with plastic wrap and refrigerate until firm, approximately 15 minutes.

5. Melt the milk chocolate, temper (Steps 4 and 5, page 179), and dip each caramel into the tempered melted chocolate with a dipping fork so that each square is completely covered with chocolate. (Turn with a fork, if necessary.) Place each dipped caramel on a baking pan lined with parchment and allow the chocolate to harden.

6. Decorate the caramels: Melt the dark chocolate in the top of a double boiler, stirring occasionally with a wooden spoon. Cut a sheet of parchment into a triangle approximately 10 × 10 × 14 inches. Roll it into a pastry bag and fill it halfway with melted dark chocolate. Cut off a tiny opening at the tip of the pastry bag and squeeze out the chocolate, drawing 2 vertical lines on each chocolate square and then 1 line horizontally so that the front of the candy looks like a wrapped package.

HINT FROM THE CHEF: Tempering dark chocolate requires precision. It is advisable for beginners to temper milk chocolate only. Test the tempered chocolate by dipping a toothpick into it to determine the length of time it takes to set. If it does not set in 2 minutes, the chocolate is not ready. Always keep chocolates in a cool, dry place. Humidity is the enemy of chocolate.

YIELD: 50 CANDIES

Culinary artistry soars to Olympian heights in this dazzling, decadent chocolate soufflé, one of the most sublime I have tasted. A surprisingly light, moist chocolate confronts you. Valrhona chocolate works best for this sumptuous dessert because it is one of the purest chocolates and has a higher cocoa content than most others.

CHOCOLATE SOUFFLE

THE QUILTED GIRAFFE

4¹/₂ ounces Valrhona (dark French) chocolate

4¹/₂ tablespoons sweet butter

2 pinches of kosher salt

2¹/₂ egg yolks

4 tablespoons very warm water

1 cup egg whites (approximately 8 to 10 whites)

¹/₄ cup sugar plus additional for sprinkling molds

2 drops freshly squeezed lemon juice

GARNISH

confectioners' sugar

1 pint espresso ice cream

¹/₂ cup whipped heavy cream

1. Preheat the oven to 450 degrees F.

2. Melt the chocolate and butter with a pinch of salt in the top of a double boiler over medium heat.

3. Whip the egg yolks and water with an electric mixer at high speed until they increase in volume by six times.

4. In another bowl, whip the egg whites at a medium speed (number 5) until frothy. Add the sugar, pinch of salt, and lemon juice slowly and beat until stiff peaks form.

5. Pour the melted chocolate into the whipped egg yolks and mix gently until homogenized.

6. Quickly add the chocolate-egg mixture to the whipped whites and fold gently together to incorporate.

7. Butter nine 3-inch soufflé molds and sprinkle them with sugar. (If the molds are buttered and sugared in advance, they should be refrigerated prior to use.) Divide the soufflé base among the molds; the mixture should be slightly higher than the top of the molds. Even the tops with a knife and bake the soufflés for 6 to 8 minutes.

8. To serve, puncture a hole in the center of each soufflé with a teaspoon. Sprinkle with confectioners' sugar and place a small scoop of espresso ice cream and whipped cream in each hole. Serve immediately.

HINTS FROM THE CHEF: The chocolate must be at the right temperature to make the perfect soufflé. If it is too hot, it will reduce the volume of the egg whites and the soufflé. The soufflé is ready when the edges turn a slightly darker shade of brown.

SERVES 9

*This chocolate mousse sensation,
sandwiched between layers of
crunchy chocolate meringue, is
named after the Place de la
Concorde, the historic square in
Paris that abuts the Gardens of the
Tuileries. The dessert requires
systematic preparation to achieve
the perfect meringue consistency and
artistry to decoratively grace the top
with chocolate meringue bits.*

*At The Palm Court, guests are
greeted with violins playing
Tchaikovsky waltzes, gilded urns,
fanning palms, and radiant
chandeliers. I have a particular
fondness for The Palm Court since
my grandparents took me to this
majestic room for strawberries and
cake when I was a child.*

CONCORD CAKE

THE PALM COURT AT THE PLAZA

CHOCOLATE MERINGUE
1 cup egg whites (approximately 8 to 10
   egg whites), cold
$^{1}/_{2}$ cup granulated sugar
$2^{1}/_{8}$ cups confectioners' sugar
2 tablespoons unsweetened cocoa powder

CHOCOLATE MOUSSE FILLING
14 ounces imported bittersweet chocolate
$^{1}/_{2}$ pound sweet butter, cut into bits,
   softened

$^{1}/_{2}$ cup absolutely fresh egg yolks
   (approximately 4 to 5 extra large egg
   yolks), at room temperature
6 egg whites, cold
$^{1}/_{2}$ cup granulated sugar

CAKE TOPPING
confectioners' sugar
imported unsweetened cocoa powder

1. Make the chocolate meringue: Place the egg whites in a very clean mixing bowl. Whip whites, then add the granulated sugar and continue to whip until soft peaks form. Beat for at least 20 minutes until the meringue takes on a glossy hue. Sift the confectioners' sugar and cocoa powder together to remove lumps. Gently fold the cocoa mixture into the meringue to incorporate, making sure not to overmix or the meringue will deflate.

2. Preheat the oven to 200 degrees F.

3. Line a large, absolutely flat baking pan with parchment. Draw three 8-inch circles on the paper with a pen or pencil. Turn the parchment over so that the ink or lead does not touch the meringue. Fill a pastry bag halfway with the chocolate meringue. Using a #4 tip (or one with $^{1}/_{4}$-inch diameter), press the pastry bag from the top (use the tip only as a guide) and make spirals starting from the center of the circle on the parchment. Work outward, ensuring that each coil touches the previous one. If any extra room on the baking pan remains, pipe strips that are the length of the pan. Otherwise, line another baking pan with parchment and make long strips. For each cake, you will need 3 meringue rounds plus about fifteen 10-inch strips. Bake the meringues for 6 to 8 hours or preferably overnight. Cool and reserve. If made ahead of time, wrap with plastic wrap.

4. Make the chocolate mousse filling: Melt the chocolate in the top of a double boiler. In a medium bowl, beat the softened butter until light and

fluffy, approximately 10 minutes. Beat in the yolks, scraping the sides of the bowl occasionally. Add the melted chocolate to the butter-yolk mixture and mix well to combine. In a grease-free bowl, whip the egg whites and sugar until firm peaks form, approximately 5 minutes (do not overbeat or they will be glossy). In a large bowl, fold one-quarter of the beaten egg whites into the chocolate mixture to lighten it. Then fold the chocolate mixture into the remaining egg whites. Reserve in a cool (not cold) place while preparing the meringues.

5. To assemble the concord cake: Gently remove the baked meringues from the parchment so they do not break. On an 8-inch cardboard circle, dab a small amount of mousse filling in the middle to affix the cake to the cardboard. Place 1 meringue layer, flat side down, on the circle and gently press to secure. With a metal spatula, spread enough mousse filling to make a layer the same thickness as the meringue. Distribute it evenly to the edges. Top with a second meringue layer, flat side up, and make another layer of filling spread to the edges the same thickness as the first layer. Top with the third meringue layer, flat side up and, with a large serrated knife, trim the edges of the meringue using the cardboard as a guide. Cover the sides and top of the cake as evenly as possible with the remaining mousse filling. (Alternatively, after the filling has firmed, trim the edges of the whole cake with a very sharp serrated edge prior to covering the cake entirely with the remaining mousse filling.)

6. Remove the strips of meringue from the parchment and press them vertically around sides of the cake, touching one another. The strips should be approximately the height of the cake. Loosely sprinkle the top of the cake to completely cover with $1/4$-inch pieces of meringue.

7. Generously sprinkle the cake with confectioners' sugar, then with cocoa powder. Refrigerate until ready to serve.

HINT FROM THE CHEF: The key to preparing this cake is to bring the egg whites, yolks, butter, and melted chocolate to room temperature before mixing them. If the butter is cold, it will solidify the chocolate.

YIELD: 1 CAKE

Many consider a meal at Lutèce to be the ultimate French dining experience in America. In fact, it has been said that French gastronomy was born in the Celtic village of Lutèce. André Soltner, the chef-proprietor, is a formidable talent in the culinary world who has garnered an extraordinary reputation for excellence. His variation on the classic frozen lemon soufflé has as its base an almond meringue, classically termed fond de succès, *which gives this dessert a wonderfully crunchy texture.*

FROZEN LEMON SOUFFLE

LUTECE

FOND DE SUCCES

5 egg whites

1 cup sugar

1 1/2 cups blanched almond flour

SOUFFLE BATTER

2 cups granulated sugar

1 cup water

10 medium egg yolks

juice and finely grated zest of 3 lemons

2 cups heavy cream, whipped

1. Preheat the oven to 200 degrees F.

2. Cut a piece of wax paper about 4 inches wide and as long as the circumference of an 8-inch soufflé dish and place it around the outer rim of the dish. Secure both ends together with tape. (The wax paper should extend 3 inches above the dish.)

3. Make the *fond de succès*: Beat the egg whites until stiff and glossy. In a bowl, mix together the sugar and almond flour and with a spatula gently fold in the egg whites. Place this meringue in a pastry bag fitted with a 1/2-inch round tip. Line a baking sheet with parchment and on it draw 2 circles a little smaller than the diameter of the soufflé dish. Turn over the parchment so that ink or lead doesn't touch the meringue. Starting in the center, make spirals outward with the meringue mixture to make the *succès*. Bake the meringues in the oven for 1 1/2 hours. Cool them in a dry place and if you are making them a day in advance, place them in a box to prevent humidity from damaging them.

4. Make the soufflé batter: In a saucepan over low heat, combine the sugar and water and cook until the temperature reaches 260 degrees F., approximately 30 minutes. When the sugar crackles, the mixture is hot enough. Beat the egg yolks with a mixer until light and fluffy, approximately 10 minutes. Pour the sugar syrup over the egg yolks while continuing to beat until the mixture cools, approximately 10 additional minutes. Using a plastic spatula, stir in the lemon juice and grated lemon zest. Fold in the whipped cream so there are no streaks, making sure to avoid overmixing.

5. Pour the batter into the prepared soufflé dish, alternating layers of *fond de succès* meringue with the batter. Cover the dish with wax paper and place it in the freezer for at least 3 hours.

6. To serve, remove the wax paper collar. Using a knife blade, score a crisscross pattern on the top of the soufflé. Slice, and serve each portion in a pool of raspberry purée garnished with a few raspberries.

SERVES 8 TO 10

CANTALOUPE SORBET WITH CHOCOLATE SEEDS

J O J O

2 cups water

1¹/₂ cups sugar

1 cantaloupe

juice of 1 lemon

2 ounces Valrhona chocolate, or other fine
    bittersweet chocolate

GARNISH

1 bunch mint

This melon sorbet dotted with chocolate seeds and served in a frozen melon rind is as tasty as it is beautiful. Similar attractive sorbet presentations can be made with pears, honeydew melons, lemons, grapefruit, and oranges. For maximum flavor, choose the sweetest, ripest, seasonal fruit.

1. In a saucepan, bring the water and sugar to a boil for approximately 2 minutes, then let cool.

2. Cut the melon in half, then cut each half into quarters (you will have 8 pieces). Cut off the rinds, place them on a tray covered with parchment, and freeze.

3. Discard the seeds and place the cantaloupe in a blender or food processor and process for 10 minutes so that the pulp is juicy. Slowly add ¹/₂ cup of the syrup and the lemon juice and blend for a short time. Taste the melon mixture: if it is too sweet, add water; if too sour, add more syrup.

4. Pour the melon purée into a sorbet machine and process. If a sorbet machine is unavailable, pour the purée into a metal ice-cube tray without the divisions, and place it in the freezer. When the purée hardens, return it to the blender or food processor and blend until smooth. Refreeze and after it hardens, it will be ready to serve. If not serving immediately, place the sorbet in an airtight container and freeze.

5. Remove the melon rinds from the freezer. With a large spatula, place a serving of the sorbet in the melon rind and shape so that it looks like the melon did before you scooped out the fruit.

6. Make the chocolate seeds: Melt the chocolate in the top of a double boiler. Make a small pastry bag out of a piece of parchment and fill with melted chocolate. Snip off the tip so you can pipe 5 chocolate seeds approximately the size of watermelon seeds on each melon section.

7. To serve, place 2 melon sections on each plate so that the melon rinds touch one another in the center and the tips point outward. Garnish the center with 2 mint leaves.

This elegant poached apple exudes cinnamon-flavored ice milk, which is sandwiched between the apple lid and bottom. The ice milk, called leche merengada *and made without eggs or cream, is a tradition that has been handed down by Spanish mothers for decades. Cafés of Madrid also serve scoops of this ice milk in tall glasses of iced coffee as a refreshing summer drink.*

RED WINE APPLE WITH CINNAMON-FLAVORED ICE MILK

ELDORADO PETIT

4 red Delicious apples

4 cups Cabernet Sauvignon or other dry red wine

1 cup sugar

2 cinnamon sticks

1 orange peel

1 lemon peel

ICE MILK

1 quart milk

2 cinnamon sticks

1 lemon peel

1 teaspoon ground cinnamon

³/4 cup sugar

GARNISH

4 mint leaves

1. Peel the apples and cut off the tops to make lids. Core the apples and cut the bottoms so that the apples will sit evenly on a flat surface. Arrange the apples in a saucepan.

2. Combine the wine, sugar, cinnamon sticks, orange peel, and lemon peel in a small bowl and pour over the apples. Cover the top of the pan with parchment to keep in the humidity. Cook slowly over medium heat until the apples are tender, approximately 25 minutes. Cool for 5 to 6 hours in the syrup.

3. Make the ice milk: In a medium saucepan, combine the milk, cinnamon sticks, lemon peel, ground cinnamon, and sugar and bring to a boil. Remove the pan from the stove for a few minutes and then reheat and bring the mixture to a boil again. This process should be repeated three times all together. Strain the mixture, place it in an ice cream machine, and process. If you do not have an ice cream machine, pour the mixture into ice-cube trays and place them in the freezer until the mixture hardens but does not freeze. Stir the cubes diagonally with a fork and return the trays to the freezer. Repeat this process five times.

4. To serve, place each apple on a plate or in a bowl, fill each apple with ice milk, top with the lid, and garnish the lid with a mint leaf. Pour approximately 3 tablespoons of the red wine syrup on the plate or soup bowl around the apple.

NOTE: The apple must marinate in the red wine syrup for several hours to absorb the wine and take on its red hue.

SERVES 4

PEAR SORBET WITH CRISPY PEAR AND PEAR LIQUEUR

LE REGENCE

This flavorful pear sorbet drenched in pear liqueur makes a refreshing intermezzo or wondrous dessert, in keeping with the regal opulence of Le Régence, located in the four-star Plaza Athénée Hotel. The crispy pear garnish provides a crunchy texture to this otherwise soothing delicate dessert.

THE SORBET
4 pears, Bartlett or Bosc
1 quart water
1¼ cups sugar
1 vanilla bean

CRISPY PEARS
2 pears, Bartlett or Bosc
juice of 1 lemon

1½ cups Clarified Butter (page 196)

¾ cup pear eau-de-vie (e.g., Poire William)

GARNISH
½ bunch mint leaves

1. Make the sorbet: Peel and core the pears. In a large saucepan, boil the water and sugar until thick and syrupy. Add the vanilla bean and pears and cook until the pears are tender, approximately 2 hours. Remove the pears and vanilla bean and reserve the syrup. Place the pears in a blender and purée. Combine the pear purée and syrup in an ice cream machine; following the manufacturer's directions, make the sorbet. If an ice cream machine is not available, you can make *granité* instead by placing the purée and syrup mixture in an ice cube tray without dividers. Put the tray in the freezer and using an up and down motion pierce the contents every ten minutes for approximately one hour.

2. Make the crispy pears: Core the pears and cut them in half lengthwise. Cut the lengths into ¼-inch-thick slices, arrange the slices on a tray, and squeeze lemon juice over them to prevent discoloration. In a warm frying pan over low heat, melt the clarified butter; add the pear slices and cook until crisp. Transfer the cooked slices to paper towels to absorb the excess butter.

3. To serve, scoop one spoonful of the sorbet into the center of a martini glass or compote and place a pear slice vertically on each side. Fill the glass with pear *eau-de-vie* until it reaches halfway up the sorbet. Garnish with mint leaves.

SERVES 6

BASICS

This classic French brioche can be baked in either a loaf pan or in brioche molds and may be used to make French toast or bread pudding. With capers and dill added to the dough, the brioche becomes a perfect accompaniment to gravlax.

BRIOCHE

HALCYON

1 ounce active dry yeast	EGG WASH
1 cup milk, lukewarm	1 egg yolk
2 cups bread flour	1 tablespoon water
$^1/_4$ cup sugar	
3 eggs	$^1/_4$ cup Clarified Butter (page 196),
1 teaspoon salt	to grease the pans
$^1/_2$ cup sweet butter, melted	
vegetable oil, to grease the bowl	

1. In a large mixing bowl, dissolve the yeast in the lukewarm milk. Let it stand for 5 minutes. Whisk in $^3/_8$ cup of the bread flour and combine well until the mixture has the consistency of a sponge. Cover the bowl with a damp towel and let the "sponge" rise in a warm place for at least 30 minutes.

2. Add the remaining flour, sugar, eggs, and salt and with electric mixer knead slowly with a dough hook until all the ingredients are well blended. Mix on medium speed for 5 minutes, until the dough slaps off the sides of the bowl. Add the melted butter in a steady stream and beat well. (The dough should be soft and a little sticky.) Let the dough rise again in a warm oiled bowl covered with plastic wrap until it doubles in volume, approximately 30 to 40 minutes. Punch the dough down and place it, covered with plastic wrap, in the refrigerator overnight.

3. Make the egg wash: Whisk the egg yolk with the water.

4. Scale and shape the dough into the desired brioche size (14-ounce oval piece for a 10- × 4-inch loaf pan, 1$^1/_2$-ounce round pieces for individual brioche molds, or three 10-ounce round flat pieces for 6-inch round cake pans used for making brioche toast). Butter the molds, loaf pan, or cake pans with clarified butter. To prepare the dough for individual brioche tins, roll it into balls, making an impression to create a $^1/_2$-inch round head attached to the rest of the dough. Pull the larger part of the dough apart to make a hole in the middle, and pull the small head through the hole. To make the loaf pan or round brioche, roll into desired form. Dust the dough with flour as needed to prevent sticking to the work surface. Brush the brioche dough with egg wash, cover with a damp cloth, and let the dough rise again until doubled in size, approximately 45 minutes.

5. Preheat the oven to 375 degrees F. Brush the brioches again with the egg wash when you are ready to place them in the oven. For brioche loaves, bake for approximately 20 minutes; for the individual brioche molds, bake approximately 10 to 15 minutes; and for the brioches made in 6-inch cake pans, bake 15 to 20 minutes or until golden brown. To test if the brioches are ready, remove them from their pans and tap them on the bottom. They should sound hollow.

HINTS FROM THE CHEF: To make a caper-dill brioche loaf, add $1/2$ cup capers and $1/8$ cup finely chopped dill to the dough after it mixes for 5 minutes in Step 2. Whether using the machine or kneading by hand, mix only to incorporate, flouring the dough as needed and making sure to push the capers into the dough so that they won't burn when you bake the brioche. After the brioche is ready, slice and toast and serve with gravlax and mustard sauce.

YIELD: TWO 10- × 4-INCH LOAVES, 21 INDIVIDUAL BRIOCHES, OR 3 ROUND LOAVES

CLARIFIED BUTTER

ARCADIA

1 cup (2 sticks) sweet butter

1. Cut the butter into small pieces and place in a heavy saucepan over moderate heat. When the pieces have melted, boil the liquid gently until you can clearly see the bottom of the pan.

2. Remove the pan from the heat and with a metal spoon skim off the foamy particles that have risen to the top.

3. Line a fine-mesh sieve with dampened cheesecloth and strain the clear yellow liquid into a small bowl. The residue that remains in the sieve can be used to enrich sauces and soups.

NOTE: Clarified butter can be stored, tightly covered, in the refrigerator, for up to 1 month.

YIELD: ABOUT ¼ CUP

CREME FRAICHE

ARCADIA

2 cups heavy cream
3 tablespoons buttermilk

Combine the heavy cream with the buttermilk in a mixing bowl. Pour the mixture into a ceramic container. Cover with plastic wrap and place in a warm place for 24 hours. Refrigerate until ready to use.

YIELD: 2 CUPS

DUCK CONFIT

PARK AVENUE CAFE

1¹/₂ medium Long Island ducks (or 6 legs and thighs)

8 garlic cloves, peeled and chopped

¹/₄ cup chopped thyme

6 bay leaves, crushed

MARINADE
1 bunch parsley, stemmed and chopped

1 cup shallots, peeled and chopped

3 cups rendered duck fat or lard (1 large duck)

¹/₄ cup kosher salt for dredging

1. At least a week before you wish to serve the confit, cut the duck legs with thighs off the duck carcass. Reserve legs and thighs and any excess skin and fat.

2. Make the rendered duck fat: Place the reserved fat in a pot over low heat, and simmer slowly until it melts. Strain and reserve the liquid. (If duck fat is unavailable or if not enough fat is rendered from the duck, rendered fat or lard can be purchased.)

3. Make the marinade: In a small bowl, combine the parsley, shallots, garlic, thyme, and bay leaves. Mix well and spread half the mixture over the bottom of a shallow roasting pan. Coat the ducks well with salt and place them on top of the marinade. Rub them with the remaining marinade. Cover and refrigerate for 4 days. Remove the marinade from the duck with a towel.

4. Heat the duck fat in a large heavy casserole over medium heat. When the fat is warm and liquefied, add the ducks and cover. Simmer for 2 to 3 hours until the meat almost falls off the bone. Remove the ducks from the pot and store in a heavy ceramic pot, completely covering the meat with duck fat. Cover and let cool to room temperature, then refrigerate.

5. When you are ready to use the confit, bring it to room temperature for several hours until the fat softens. Remove the duck pieces and wipe off the excess fat.

HINTS FROM THE CHEF: If you are unable to make the rendered duck fat, you can purchase lard in a commercial supermarket, or you can purchase duck confit or rendered duck fat from D'Artagnan in New Jersey by calling 1(800) DARTAGN.

SERVES 6

This splendid and flavorful recipe originated in Gascony, a region in southwestern France known for such other delicacies as foie gras *and* magret, *the chewy breast of fattened moulard duck. The tradition of cooking and storing duck in its own fat in earthenware pots derived from the Moors, who once passed through this part of France. Duck and goose confit were made during World War II in places where there was little refrigeration, since the rendered fat serves as a preservative for the meat.*

HERB OILS

LA CARAVELLE AND MONTRACHET

1 CUP CHILI OIL
  (La Caravelle)
1 cup vegetable oil
1 fresh red chili pepper
zest of 1 lime
1 teaspoon soy sauce

1 CUP BASIL OIL
  (La Caravelle)
1 cup extra-virgin olive oil
2 tablespoons chopped basil
1 vitamin C tablet

1 CUP RED PEPPER OIL
  (Montrachet)
2 red bell peppers, roasted and seeded
1/2 cup olive oil

salt and freshly ground black pepper to taste

1 1/2 CUPS DILL OIL
  (La Caravelle)
1 cup extra-virgin olive oil
4 tablespoons chopped dill
1 vitamin C tablet

1 CUP ROSEMARY OIL
  (La Caravelle)
1 cup extra-virgin olive oil
1 sprig rosemary

Make the chili oil: In a blender or food processor, process well the vegetable oil, red chili pepper, lime zest, and soy sauce. Strain through a fine-mesh sieve or *chinois* into a squeeze bottle. Let the ingredients infuse, refrigerated, overnight.

Make the basil oil: In a blender or food processor, process the olive oil, basil, and vitamin C for 30 seconds. Strain through a fine-mesh sieve or *chinois* into a squeeze bottle and let the ingredients infuse, refrigerated, overnight.

Make the red pepper oil: Place the roasted peppers in a food processor and process until smooth. Slowly drizzle in the olive oil and process until smooth. Season with salt and pepper. Strain through a fine-mesh sieve or *chinois* into a squeeze bottle and let the ingredients infuse, refrigerated, overnight.

Make the dill oil: In a blender or food processor, process the oil, dill, and the vitamin C tablet. Strain the mixture through a fine-mesh sieve or *chinois* into a squeeze bottle. Let the ingredients infuse, refrigerated, overnight.

Make the rosemary oil: Pour the oil into a jar, add the rosemary, and let the oil stand for at least 2 days at room temperature before using.

NOTE: A vitamin C tablet is added to some oils to preserve the green color.

WHOLE WHEAT PAPPARDELLE

FELIDIA

3¹/₂ cups whole wheat flour plus extra
   for dusting
2 eggs

¹/₂ teaspoon salt
1 teaspoon olive oil
¹/₂ cup warm water

1. Place the flour on a marble or wooden surface and make a well in the center. Beat the eggs and salt and pour them into the well, using your fingers to incorporate half of the flour. After half has been incorporated, stir in the olive oil. Flour your hands to remove the sticky pieces of dough and add the warm water to the flour and incorporate.

2. Knead the dough by hand for 10 minutes or use the kneading hook in an electric mixer until the dough is smooth and shaped like a ball. Add additional flour if the dough becomes too sticky, or water if it becomes too firm. Cover the dough with plastic wrap and refrigerate for 2 hours.

3. Cut the dough into 3 pieces. On a lightly floured surface, roll 1 piece of the dough at a time. Roll away from you and around the rolling pin until thin. Feed the dough through the second narrowest opening of a pasta machine. Cut the dough into 1-inch-wide strips the length of the rolling pin, then cut them into 1- × 5-inch strips. Repeat this process with the remaining dough. Place the individual pappardelle strips on a floured sheet pan overnight to dry.

4. In a large soup pot, bring 6 quarts of salted water to a rapid boil. Add the pappardelle, stirring the pasta as you drop it into the water. Cook for approximately 1¹/₂ minutes, or until *al dente*. Drain the pasta well.

HINTS FROM THE CHEF: You can use the same ingredients to make other pasta shapes, including *pasutice* (these look like 2-inch lozenges), *fuzi* (*pasutice* that have been rolled around the tip of the left index finger to form "quill" shapes), *taglioline* (spaghetti), and *tagliatelli* (like fettuccine).

YIELD: 1 POUND

This classic soft white dinner roll is particularly tasty sprinkled with sesame seeds.

PARKER HOUSE ROLLS

PARK AVENUE CAFE

$1^1/_2$ ounces baker's or brewer's yeast

$^3/_8$ cup warm water

1 cup milk

4 tablespoons butter, cut into bits

3 tablespoons sugar

$3^1/_2$ cups sifted all-purpose flour

$^1/_2$ teaspoon salt

TOPPING

$^1/_8$ cup butter, melted

1 egg white

coarse salt for sprinkling

3 tablespoons black and white sesame
  seeds

1. In a small bowl, combine the yeast and the water, mixing until the yeast dissolves. Proof until bubbles form on the water's surface.

2. Place the milk, butter, and sugar in a saucepan over low heat and warm until the butter melts halfway, stirring occasionally. Remove the pan from the heat, stirring until the butter is completely melted and just warm to the touch. Add the dissolved yeast and stir. Let mixture cool to room temperature.

3. In an electric mixer, combine 3 cups flour and the salt in a bowl, add the milk/yeast mixture, and mix on the lowest speed with the dough hook until the batter becomes elastic. Then add the remaining $^1/_2$ cup flour and mix for a few minutes at medium speed until well incorporated. Remove the dough from the bowl and knead with your hands several times by pressing and folding it in half until the dough is smooth. Place the dough in a stainless steel bowl and cover with a wet cloth or plastic wrap so that it does not form a coating. Optional: brush the dough with vegetable oil. Let the dough "proof" (rise) in a warm place until it doubles in size, approximately 30 to 45 minutes. Punch the dough down to release the air. Let the dough rest in the bowl for an additional 15 minutes.

4. Cut the dough in half and then in eighths. Roll into sixteen 2-ounce balls approximately 2 inches in diameter. Butter four 5-inch loaf pans and place 4 balls in each loaf pan. Brush the top of each roll with melted butter. Whisk the egg white until frothy and then brush the tops of the rolls with the egg white and sprinkle with coarse salt followed by sesame seeds. Let proof until the dough doubles in size, approximately 20 minutes. (Alternatively, to make loaves, roll dough into 2 large oval pieces approximately 10 × 4 inches. Butter two 10- × 4-inch loaf pans and let proof until the dough doubles in size, approximately 30 to 45 minutes.)

5. Preheat the oven to 350 degrees F.

6. Bake the rolls for approximately 20 minutes or bake the loaves for 30 minutes, until golden brown. Remove the rolls from the pans immediately and let them cool on a rack.

N O T E :   To determine whether the rolls are done, remove one from the pan, hold it up to your ear, and tap the bottom. If you hear a hollow sound, then it is done. If not, a lot of moisture and raw dough remain, and the rolls will require additional baking.

Y I E L D :   1 6   R O L L S   O R   2   P O U N D S   O F   D O U G H

RAVIOLI

I L   N I D O

3¹/₂ cups durum flour, plus extra for
  dusting
¹/₂ cup semolina flour
8 eggs

E G G   W A S H
1–2 eggs, beaten

1. Place the flours on a wooden or marble surface, make a well in the center of the flour, and add the eggs to the well. Blend them by hand to form a dough and shape the dough into a ball.

2. Roll the dough into thin sheets on a floured surface with a rolling pin or in a pasta machine. Let the dough rest for 10 minutes. Spray the sheets with water, then brush them with the egg wash. Using a 2¹/₂-inch round or square cutter with a fluted edge, cut the dough into 2-inch squares.

3. Dust the ravioli squares with flour and fill them according to the recipe you are using.

4. In a large pot, bring 1 tablespoon of olive oil and 4 quarts of salted water to a rolling boil. Add the ravioli and cook until *al dente*, about 3 minutes. Drain the pasta immediately in a colander or, if you are making it ahead of time, rinse it with cold water to stop the cooking process.

Y I E L D :   2   P O U N D S   R A V I O L I   D O U G H

PUFF PASTRY

LUTECE

1 pound Wondra flour, sifted
1¹/₂ teaspoons salt

1 pound unsalted butter, chilled, cut into
 bits
³/₄ cup very cold water

1. Sift the flour and salt into a mixing bowl or the bowl of a food processor. Add 3 tablespoons of butter and blend well by hand or in a food processor by pulsing 10 times. Gradually incorporate just enough water to hold the dough together. The mixture should resemble coarse meal.

2. Remove the dough from the bowl and place it on a lightly floured work surface. Work the dough with the heel of your hand to form a ball. Cut an **X** on the top of the ball. Cover the dough with plastic wrap and refrigerate for at least one hour.

3. Meanwhile, on a lightly floured sheet of wax paper, knead the remaining butter into a pliable, round 6-inch form. Refrigerate.

4. Place the dough in the center of a lightly floured sheet of wax paper and pull each corner of the **X** section outward to form a 12-inch square. Place the butter in the center of the dough and fold the dough corners over the butter so that the corners meet in the center. Turn the dough over seam side down and roll out into a 12-inch × 18-inch rectangle.

5. Starting with the short end, crease the dough vertically into three sections. Fold the top section downward and the bottom section upward so that it looks like a business letter. Turn the dough 90 degrees clockwise, roll the dough again into a rectangle, and repeat the folding process. Make sure not to roll the pin over the ends of the dough or the butter will ooze out. Wrap in plastic wrap and chill for one hour.

6. Roll the dough into a 12-inch × 18-inch rectangle and repeat Step 5 two additional times (for a total of 6 turns). Make sure to chill the dough each time. It will then be ready for forming and baking according to your recipe instructions.

YIELD: 2 POUNDS

LIGHT CHICKEN STOCK

PARK AVENUE CAFE

5 pounds chicken bones, cut into 3-inch
   pieces

6 quarts water

2 onions, peeled and quartered

1 carrot, peeled and cut into 3 pieces

1/2 bunch celery, including leaves, roughly
   chopped

12 peppercorns

1 bay leaf

sea salt to taste

1. Rinse the chicken bones and in a large soup pot combine them with all the remaining ingredients.

2. Bring the mixture to a boil and simmer for 3 hours, skimming off the foam every half hour.

3. Line a fine-mesh sieve with dampened cheesecloth and set it over a large bowl. Ladle the liquid into the sieve and then wring out the cheesecloth over the bowl. Let the stock cool.

4. Refrigerate the stock in a storage container and when the fat hardens remove it from the top.

HINT FROM THE CHEF: To make Dark Chicken Stock, follow the recipe up to Step 4. Then return the stock to the pot and simmer it over low heat until it is reduced to 2 cups, approximately 45 minutes. Let it cool, then refrigerate the stock in a storage container. When the fat hardens remove it from the top.

YIELD: 4 QUARTS

FISH STOCK

HARRY CIPRIANI

2–3 pounds bones and trimmings from
 any white fish
1 medium onion, peeled and cut into
 chunks
2 leeks, white part only, thoroughly
 washed and sliced
1 stalk celery, cut into chunks
2 quarts cold water
1 cup dry white wine
juice of $1/2$ lemon

1 teaspoon salt
bouquet garni tied in cheesecloth:
 1 head garlic, unpeeled but punctured
  in 3 places with the tip of a knife,
  or halved
 3 sprigs Italian parsley
 1 sprig thyme
 1 bay leaf
 1 black peppercorn

1. Combine all the ingredients in a soup pot and bring the mixture to a boil over high heat. Skim off the foam that rises to the top and reduce the heat to medium. Cook, partially covered, for 20 minutes (all together the fish stock should cook for at least 1 hour). Strain the mixture through a fine-mesh sieve set over a bowl.

2. Let the stock cool, then refrigerate it, covered. Remove the fat from the chilled stock prior to use. The stock may be stored in the refrigerator for 2 to 3 days or in the freezer for 1 month.

YIELD: 2 QUARTS

GAME STOCK

T H E ' 2 1 ' C L U B

*2 pounds poultry bones (quail, duck, or
chicken), necks and wing tips*

2 carrots, peeled and coarsely chopped

1 onion, peeled and coarsely chopped

3 stalks celery, coarsely chopped

1 bay leaf

1/2 bunch thyme, stems only

1 garlic clove, peeled

1 quart water

1 quart Brown Veal Stock (page 207)

1. Preheat the oven to 375 degrees F.

2. Place the poultry bones in an oiled roasting pan and roast them in the oven
until nicely browned, approximately 40 minutes.

3. Place the browned bones, vegetables, the bay leaf, thyme, and garlic clove
in a large stockpot and cover with the water and veal stock. Bring the
mixture to a boil over high heat, lower the heat, and simmer for 2 hours,
until the mixture has reduced by half. Remove the stock from the heat and
let it cool. Pour the stock through a fine-mesh sieve into a bowl and cool.
Store the stock, covered, in the refrigerator for 1 or 2 days, or in the freezer
for up to 1 month.

Y I E L D : 1 Q U A R T

SHELLFISH STOCK

AUREOLE

3 pounds lobster and/or shrimp shells

¹/₄ cup plus 2 tablespoons olive or
    vegetable oil

3 carrots, peeled and chopped

³/₄ head celery, chopped

1 bulb fennel, chopped

2 medium onions, peeled and chopped

1 head garlic, cloves peeled

2 cups dry white wine

³/₄ pound fresh or canned plum tomatoes,
    peeled and chopped

1 quart Fish Stock (page 204)

1 quart Light Chicken Stock (page
    203), or water

1 teaspoon dried thyme

6 black peppercorns

1 bay leaf

1. Preheat the oven to 400 degrees F. Place the lobster and/or shrimp shells in a roasting pan, pour ¹/₄ cup of oil over them, and roast for 25 minutes.

2. Meanwhile, in a saucepan, heat 2 tablespoons of oil and sweat the *mirepoix* of carrots, celery, fennel, and onions over medium heat. When almost translucent, add garlic cloves and cook for an additional 10 minutes.

3. Place the lobster and/or shrimp shells in a large soup pot. (If using lobsters, smash the backs.) Add the *mirepoix* and deglaze the pot with white wine. Reduce over medium heat for approximately 15 minutes or until the liquid almost evaporates.

4. Add the tomatoes and fish and chicken stocks to the soup pot and bring to a boil. Skim off the scum, and add the thyme, peppercorns, and bay leaf. Simmer uncovered for 1¹/₄ hours, skimming off the scum from time to time.

5. Strain the stock through a fine-mesh sieve or *chinois* set over a bowl. Let the stock cool, then refrigerate covered until ready to use. You may store the stock in the freezer for up to a month.

YIELD: 1¹/₄ QUARTS

BROWN VEAL STOCK

LA COTE BASQUE

4 pounds veal bones

5 quarts water

4 medium carrots, peeled and diced

5 medium onions, peeled and diced

3–4 medium stalks celery, diced

3 leeks, green parts only

5 garlic cloves, peeled and halved

1/2 cup tomato purée

2 bay leaves

2 teaspoons dried thyme, crumbled

5 black peppercorns

Classic French veal stock is a mainstay of the great French sauces as well as those of a variety of other cuisines. This flavorful and aromatic stock develops its amber color from the roasting of the veal bones and the addition of tomato purée.

1. Preheat the oven to 400 degrees F. Place the veal bones in a large oiled roasting pan and roast them in the oven for 1 hour.

2. Transfer the bones to an 8-quart stockpot. Deglaze the roasting pan by adding 2 cups of the water and scraping the pan to loosen the brown bits sticking to the bottom. Add these pan juices to the pot along with the vegetables, garlic, tomato purée, bay leaves, thyme, and peppercorns. Cover the mixture with the remaining water and simmer for about 4 hours, skimming the surface occasionally with a spoon to remove the foam and adding more water as necessary.

3. Strain the stock through a fine colander into a large bowl, pressing on the vegetables to extract all the liquid. Discard the bones and vegetables. Cool and store tightly covered in the refrigerator or freezer. The stock can be refrigerated for 2 to 3 days or frozen for up to 1 month.

YIELD: 3 QUARTS

In a restaurant kitchen, there is a ready supply of vegetable parts for making this stock. However, you may use any vegetable parts— stems, roots, or leaves (except broccoli stems)—for flavor. Add fennel and celeriac if available as they will add wonderfully assertive tastes.

VEGETABLE STOCK

THE SEA GRILL

2 quarts water

3 carrots, peeled and chopped

1 leek, root only, very well washed

2 onions, unpeeled but cubed

5 garlic cloves, peeled

2 bunches scallions, green parts and roots only

1 bunch dill stems and/or leaves

1 bunch Italian parsley stems

2 bay leaves

12 cracked peppercorns

1 dried chili pepper, with seeds

sea salt and freshly ground black pepper

In a large stockpot, bring 2 quarts of water to a boil and add all the vegetables. Simmer, uncovered, for 25 minutes. Add the herbs and spices and simmer an additional 5 minutes. Strain the mixture through a colander into a bowl, season with salt and pepper to taste, let cool, then store, covered, in the refrigerator or freezer.

YIELD: 1 QUART

RECIPE LISTING

(BY RESTAURANT)

INDEX